THE
RESTLESSNESS
OF THE CALL

6-08

many

Carry the

Fire!

McDougal & Associates
Servants of Christ and stewards of the mysteries of God

Favored!

You are a mighty woman of God!

THE RESTLESSNESS OF THE CALL

OF THE CALL

Remaining Faithful through the
Process of Being Appointed,
Anointed, and Prepared

By

Mary Cummings

Original cover design by Lara York
zoecreationgrafx@bellsouth.net

Published by:

McDougal & Associates
P.O. Box 194
Greenwell Springs, LA 70739-0194
www.thepublishedword.com

McDougal & Associates is dedicated to the spreading of the Gospel of Jesus Christ to as many people as possible in the shortest time possible.

ISBN 0-9777053-1-5

Printed in the United States of America
For Worldwide Distribution

DEDICATION

I dedicate this book to my parents, John and Mildred Rose. The outstanding Christian heritage I received from these godly parents has brought me many blessings. Their strength, compassion, and undying love for God has not only affected me, but will also affect many generations to come.

A Note to Bible Lovers

When I read something, I love to see its relationship to the Scriptures, and I know that many of you feel the same way. When I wrote *The Restlessness of the Call,* I generously interspersed the text with Bible references, showing the source of my various thoughts. I find that to be very convenient when I want to study a matter further.

There are many others, however, possibly a majority, who find Bible references strung out between words and phrases of the text of the book to be very instrusive to the message, and that's what's important to them. They would rather read the message without the interruption of the biblical sources and deal with those later.

In the end, I have tried to reach a suitable compromise. All of the biblical references originally inserted within the text are listed at the end of the book in an Endnote section, and the spots they previously occupied are numbered for your convenience. For all those who love to study God's Word, this should provide a treasure-trove of resource material.

CONTENTS

FOREWORD BY REV. W. HAROLD BAGNETTO

The Restlessness of the Call could be the title of Mary Cummings' life story. She always knew that God had called her for a purpose, but many events in her life and her position as wife, mother and, often, provider for her family, seemed to limit her ability to pursue certain areas of ministry. Still, ministry seemed to find her, and the anointing to go with it was there.

Since 1993, when I first met Mary (I've been her pastor now for nearly fourteen years), I can say that she's been just that, restless for the call of God, knowing there was something special He had for her to do and not wanting to miss it. When a door opened, she wasn't about to let it pass.

A revival that swept our area in the mid to late 1990s brought to Mary a fresh appetite for more, and it wasn't long before God had begun to open doors for her at conferences, retreats, and other special services, where she was able to share fresh fire with those who were hungry. Healings and manifestations of the presence of God have consistently followed her ministry.

If anyone knows what it's like to have a word or calling from God and then have to wait patiently for it to come to fruition, it's Mary Cummings. Because of that, I believe you will enjoy the message of this book and that it will bring to you new insight into the calling of God and its fulfillment for your own life.

Rev. W. Harold Bagnetto
Pastor
The Healing Place at Glad Tidings
Shreveport, Louisiana

FOREWORD BY REV. J. MONTY DUKE, JR.

Thank you, Sister Mary, for being obedient to the Lord and giving us solid Christian truths for our lives today. You have brought us insight into the spirit realm, revealing that each person has a unique destiny and is called to fulfill God's will in their life, and that He never calls anyone to fail. You have shown us that we can only achieve true success through His plan and by our faithfulness to Him.

With godly wisdom, you have revealed that He demands loyalty and obedience through the humility of a repentant heart, and that He will do the miraculous for all those who will follow His prescribed pathway.

Rev. J. Monty Duke, Jr.
President and Founder,
Jesus Set me Free Ministry, Inc.
Founder and Executive Pastor,
Open Door Revival Center,
Cut Off, Louisiana

FOREWORD BY REV. MIRIAM H. BERTHELOT

I have co-labored with Mary Cummings over the past twelve years and watched as her ministry developed, and, because of that, I can say that she is a unique woman of God. Mary has a two-fold anointing. She operates in the priestly anointing as a minister and in the kingly anointing as a business woman. I have also seen her take the sacred things of the Word of God and apply them to the business world to enable men and women to understand the practical things of God.

Mary's book, *The Restlessness of the Call,* reveals how great men of God of biblical times struggled with the everyday details of life, just as we do today. Some of them came out victorious, while others failed. What a message of hope this is for the everyday person! We can all be successful in the things of God.

Rev. Miriam H. Berthelot
Co-Pastor
Crossroads Assembly of God
Blanchard, Louisiana
Former Director of Women's Ministries Unlimited
Louisiana District of the Assemblies of God

Foreword by Jeff R. Fendley

Most Christians struggle with God's call upon their lives, for the process of discerning His will is never easy. While we may have an overall vision of where He is leading us, we sometimes fail to find His direction in the daily walk of faith. Because God's plans are seldom what we expect, we can easily become discouraged and confused in the process.

This book, *The Restlessness of the Call,* will help you to better understand God's ways so that you can more clearly see and follow His path. In the book, Mary Cummings shares rich insight from Old Testament characters who also struggled with God's call. She reminds us that God will complete the work He has started in each of us, if we are obedient and stay submitted to His will.

Through reading this book, you'll be both challenged and blessed in your own walk with God.

Jeff Fendley
Director of Training
Merry Maids Home Office
Memphis, Tennessee

I know the plans I have for you, declares the Lord, ... plans to give you hope and a future ... .

You will seek me and find me when you seek me with all your heart.

Jeremiah 29:11 and 13, NIV

INTRODUCTION

When I was ten years old, the Lord placed the world into my heart, and I have had a heart for missions ever since. All of us are born with a purpose. We are created, first of all, to have fellowship with God and to worship Him.

God also gives us all the privilege of being fishers of men, of discipling others to serve Him. Still, each person possesses personal God-given gifts that work with their specific calling, a calling designed to impact the world in some particular way for Christ. Such gifts and special abilities are displayed in childhood, but, at that point in time, they're usually not yet seen in the way God intends to use them in the future. Each of us has something unusual and specific to look forward to in life.

How can we explain these unique and individual gifts and why one person gets one and another person gets another? We can't. We can only say that God will appoint whom He wills for His purposes. And who are we to question God?

Not every individual is willing to use their God-given gifts for the purpose for which they were intended, but true Christians are always eager to do what God wants them to. They seek His will in prayer and, in time, He makes their specific call real to them. This sometimes happens through a prophetic word given to them by another Christian, through a vision or dream, or just through something we might call an inward knowing. When a person feels they've heard from God about their call and they decide to say *yes* to that call, it's a very exciting time. They find great peace in the knowledge that they're in the perfect will of God.

But usually what is envisioned at this point is the fullness of the established call and not the steps that will be necessary to walk into that call. There is always a process that brings us from the moment of appointment and anointing to the time of the fulfillment of our call. None of these steps can be avoided or skipped over, if we are to move toward the goal of eventual establishment.

The problem is that it's sometimes difficult to understand God's processes. *What is God doing now?* we often wonder. Is this current incident a part of the needed preparation? Or is this simply a distraction? We need to know, and not knowing sometimes leads to discouragement and even failure.

Accepting God's call is just a first step. It's then that the real training begins, and that period of training is not always an easy one. Daily walking in obedience to God, even while in training, is just as great a part of being in God's will as is the final outcome.

God uses other people for the purpose of shaping us, and we must be willing for their participation. Being submitted to others is often the same as being submitted to God.

Another problem we face is understanding God's timetable. It seems to take so long for His plan to finally happen.

When we respond to the call, it seems that we are then tossed as far away from it as we possibly can be, and we have to trust that the Lord will lead us ... until we eventually walk into the fulfillment of the call, at just the right time.

There is always a perfect timing involved with every call, and because of this, it's easy for us to become restless and begin to feel that the established call will never come. From time to time, God allows us to see a piece of what He's doing, and this brings encouragement and renewed hope to our spirits. Otherwise, we tend to give way to restlessness.

When restlessness comes, it can be very dangerous. For instance, we often decide not to wait for God's timing, but to try to make something happen on our own. It's not easy to trust God completely when we can't see the beginning from the end. But His call is so important to our lives that we must become determined to carefully follow His leading, so that the call will be established at the right time and in the right way.

Other people are sometimes not very helpful when it comes to our call, and this contributes to our tendency to restlessness. Family members and friends often fail to understand the call or what God has spoken to us regarding our future and purpose, and so they offer their own opinion on the matter. But God is never moved by man's opinion. He always does things according to His own plan.

Other people are often slow to cooperate with what God has said or even to recognize our call or special gifts. This can be devastating when the people involved are in leadership: in the family, in the community, and especially in the

Church. Otherwise good leaders are often guilty of failing to mentor or give opportunities to those who have special gifts and talents, when it's clearly within their power to do so. The reason is that they cannot see us as God sees us.

What should we do when this happens? It forces us into an utter dependence upon God. We know that if He doesn't do it, it won't happen. And that's not a bad thing. It can be very comforting to know that the future plan for our lives is not being directed by any other human being, but by God Himself. When we're faithful, therefore, each battle we face will bring us another victory and will move us from one level to the next, until we eventually find ourselves walking in our established call.

What are the secrets of getting there? If we are to be successful in fulfilling the call of God upon our lives, His altar cannot be bypassed or taken lightly, for seeking God's presence is a must. Our wrong attitudes and any impurities that are found in us must be dealt with, and the altar must be revisited again and again so that the heart can remain pure before the Lord. When we obey God's leading with a pure heart, His plan for us will surely emerge, and we will be so glad we were not detoured by *The Restlessness of the Call.*

Mary Cummings
Shreveport, Louisiana

PART I

TWO KINGS

CHAPTER 1

SAUL

Now there was a man of Benjamin, whose name was Kish, ... a Benjamite, a mighty man of power. And he had a son, whose name was SAUL, a choice young man, and a goodly: and there was not among the children of Israel a goodlier person than he: from his shoulders and upward he was higher than any of the people.

1 Samuel 9:1-2, Emphasis Added

This young man Saul had a rich family heritage. Jacob, the great patriarch of Israel, had twelve sons,[1] and the families of those sons came to be called the twelve tribes of Israel.[2] Benjamin, the youngest of the sons and the only full brother of Joseph,[3] was born to Jacob and his favorite wife Rachel (who died giving birth to him). Jacob already loved Joseph, and now Benjamin was very special to him too.

Jacob's name later changed to Israel, when he had an encounter with an angel at Bethel.[4] Just before Israel's death, he prophesied that the tribe of Benjamin would be made up of courageous, cunning, and determined warriors.[5] In time, the tribe of Benjamin did indeed become large, but then, because of sin, it lost many of its people and nearly became extinct.[6]

> **God was not taken by surprise by all of this!**

Saul was at least the sixth generation of the family of Benjamin. His father, Kish, was a powerful man in that tribe.[7] During Saul's lifetime, his people lived in the Promised Land, or Canaan, where Jacob had also settled,[8] and which was considered a family inheritance from God. But how was it that Saul became king?

ISRAEL WANTED A KING[9]

Hundreds of years before, Moses had prophesied that when the people came into the land, they would eventually want their own king.[10] Now, just as he had prophesied, the elders of Israel began to beg their current leader for a king. They wanted to be like other nations around them, they said.

Until that time, the nation had been ruled by a series of judges, beginning with Joshua. These were spiritual giants, men and women of deep spiritual insight. They knew how to touch God for the people, and they had no fear about administering His will. The prophet Samuel, the current judge, was understandably unhappy with this request. He felt that the people were rejecting him.

There was more to the story than that. Samuel was now old and had made his two sons, who were not walking in the ways of the Lord themselves, to be judges over Israel in his stead. These sons were doing things like taking bribes and perverting judgment. Israel clearly needed better leadership.

Samuel talked to the Lord about this request for a king, and God told him that *He* was the one being rejected by the people, not Samuel. God wanted to be the King over Israel, but if the people insisted on being like other nations, Samuel should give them their king.

God was not taken by surprise by all of this. He knew very well when and how this turn of events would come about, and He had long been preparing a man for this role. That man was Saul, the Benjamite, son of Kish.

BECOMING THE KING[11]

DIRECTED INTO DESTINY

Physically, Saul was a big man. He stood head and shoulders above the rest of his people. But he had other things going for him as well. He had favor among the people because of his reputation for kindness, compassion, and helpfulness. This was demonstrated in the event that was to bring him to the fore.

THE RESTLESSNESS OF THE CALL

One day Kish's herd of donkeys could not be found, and he asked his trusted son Saul to take a servant with him and go and look for the animals. Saul and the servant went as requested and, for the next three days, searched everywhere they could think of, but they were unable to find the wandering donkeys.

At this point, Saul was faced with a dilemma. He very much wanted to please his father by returning with the donkeys, but he was afraid that his father would begin to worry about him, and his continued absence would, thus, become a greater problem than the missing donkeys. Reluctantly, he made the decision to return home without the animals he had been sent to recover.

As the two men began their journey home, Saul remembered hearing about a prophet of God who lived nearby. It was said that whatever this prophet spoke came true. Perhaps this man could help them find the lost animals. It was worth a try.

Then Saul had another concern. If they did go to inquire of the prophet, they had nothing to give him for his services. They had run out of provisions, and Saul had no money with him. The servant said that he had one coin. If the prophet could help them, he would give him the coin. Agreed, they headed up the hill to the city to find the prophet, a man everyone called the Seer.

As they came closer to the city, they saw some young ladies going to a well to draw water, and they asked these ladies where they might find the Seer. The reply they received was a welcome one. It just so happened that the Seer had come to the city that very day to attend a special sacrifice the people were conducting at "the high place." This was a special place set aside for worship and sacrifice to the Lord. "If you hurry," the young ladies told them, "you can catch him before he goes up. But hurry. The people will be waiting for him to bless the sacrifice before they can eat."

Saul and the servant hurried into the city, and there they found a man named Samuel at the gate. He was just leaving for the high place, he said. Saul asked Samuel where the house of the Seer was and was surprised by the answer. "I am the Seer," Samuel replied. "Come up to the high place and eat with me, and tomorrow you can be on your way. I want to tell you everything that's in your heart."

Then the prophet added, "Oh, by the way, those donkeys you lost three days ago ... , don't worry about them. They've been found."

With that news, Saul relaxed and gladly accepted the invitation to dinner.

The Appointment

Samuel was not taken by surprise by this visit. God had spoken to him the day before and told him that Saul, the Benjamite, would be arriving the same time the next day. He also told Samuel that Saul was the one He had chosen to become the king of Israel. Samuel was to anoint him for that purpose. Saul's calling would be to protect the inheritance of God's people and their land from the enemy and to govern the nation in a godly way.

For Saul's part, as he went on his way searching for a herd of donkeys, he surely did not realize that he would soon have an encounter that would so dramatically change his life. He was destined to become a history maker, and his moment of destiny was at hand.

God used that herd of lost donkeys (an uncontrollable situation) to lead Saul to the right place at the appointed time, and God directed Saul to this particular city for this particular encounter. That it happened on the day of sacrifice and that the timing was so perfect that Saul would meet Samuel at the city gate were all part of God's plan. He set it all up by design.

Is it God's will that animals become lost and we have to waste time hunting them? Well, He can use that or any other circumstance to lead us into our destiny.

God set certain things in motion to bring Saul to the prophet so that the man of God could call forth Heaven's plan and purpose for him. Still, it had to be a very frustrating experience for Saul. His father had asked him to find and bring home his animals, but although he had very diligently sought them, they were nowhere to be found. Then, when he had felt that he had no other option but to go home empty handed, the idea had come to him to try one more thing. As a last resort, he had sought out the prophet, and that was the thing that led him to his destiny.

Every part of the puzzle was important, and God was in the details the whole time. And what was Saul feeling about all of this? Well, he was tired, hungry, frustrated, and perplexed, and how could he know that he was about to become the guest of honor at a feast celebrating a very different future for himself?

PREPARATIONS OF THE HEART

When the two men met, Samuel told Saul that he would tell him what was already in his heart. This shows us that something else was going on in Saul's heart, even as he sought his father's lost animals. God always prepares the willing heart for what He's about to do.

> *God set it all up by design!*

What Samuel would tell Saul, although it must have seemed impossible and beyond reason to the lad at the time, could not have come as a complete shock to him. Often, we fail to recognize or understand exactly what is happening to us or others at the moment, especially when it seems to be something we consider to be impossible.

Years before, God must have planted a seed in Saul's heart, and he must have wondered many times if that seed would ever really bear fruit. One thing is sure. He had never abandoned his dream of one day leading his nation.

The Scriptures show that Saul was a good man. Long before, God had placed within him a compassion for the people he would one day lead. It was already in his heart to take care of and protect them, and this resulted in his finding great favor with them. God knew it, Saul knew it, and now Samuel knew it. He must affirm Saul's destiny to him before he left that place.

GOD CHOOSES WHOM HE WILL

Even as he revealed to Saul that he need not be worried because his father's donkeys had been found, Samuel said something else that proved much more difficult for Saul to understand:

> *And on whom is all the desire of Israel? Is it not on thee, and on all thy father's house?* 1 Samuel 9:20

By this, Samuel meant to begin explaining to Saul that he and his family were being elevated because Israel had asked for a king. But when the conversation turned deadly serious, Saul was suddenly afraid. This man must be mistaken.

Saul quickly reminded Samuel that Benjamin was the smallest of the tribes and that his family was *"the least"* of all the families of Benjamin. According to the culture of the day, he was in the wrong family (and even in the least likely part of that wrong family) to expect any important position in the nation. In the natural realm, what the man was saying seemed impossible. But God never chooses men based on the culture of the day or the prevailing thoughts of men.

PROPHETIC ACTS PROCLAIMING THE CALL

Samuel took Saul and his servant into the house and sat Saul in a place of honor. About thirty people had been invited to the feast, and the others were already there waiting. Samuel instructed the cook to bring forth the special piece of meat he had previously ordered to be prepared. The cook brought it in and placed it before Saul.

The piece of meat in question was the shoulder of the sacrifice, a piece usually reserved for the priests, since it represented authority and spiritual leadership. Samuel explained to Saul that he had given this instruction to the cook before he had even invited the guests for the celebration. He had known Saul was coming, and God had told him just what to do.

Seating Saul in the place of honor and serving him the shoulder of the animal were prophetic acts. Samuel was showing those of earth what God's plan was. In this way, God uses men to proclaim the things of Heaven on earth and, thus, to set them in motion.

THE CALL WAS PERSONAL

Later, back in the city, Samuel continued talking to Saul on the housetop. This would be the equivalent of us inviting someone to sit with us on our porch and visit.

The following morning Samuel got Saul and his servant up early to begin their journey home. As he walked with them toward the gate of the city, Samuel asked Saul to send his servant ahead so that they could talk privately about what God had said. Saul complied, sending his servant ahead so that he and Samuel could be alone.

> **When the call of God comes, there's no room for the opinions of men!**

God had instructed Samuel to anoint Saul for the call upon his life, so he now took a flask of oil and poured it upon the young man's head and then kissed him. His declaration was powerful in its simplicity:

Is it not because the Lord hath anointed thee to be captain over his inheritance? 1 Samuel 10:1

The call of God is very personal, and when it comes, there's no room for the opinions of men. Saul did not choose this calling, but he was chosen by God. Recognizing the solemnity of this moment, Saul knelt humbly as Samuel poured the anointing oil over him. This seemingly accidental encounter had turned into a divine appointment, and the divine appointment had now turned into a divine calling.

What God had said seemed like an unimaginably

difficult assignment, but this personal anointing would mark the beginning of Saul's preparation for his new position. If he continued to be faithful to God, when the time came to serve in this capacity, he would be ready.

SIGNS THAT PROVED WHAT GOD HAD SAID

Before they parted that day, Samuel conveyed to Saul the fact that God would now give him signs (to prove to him that he had heard from Heaven) and that this was indeed the word of the Lord for his life. As he went on his way home, he would see two men beside that famous landmark that was loved and respected by all, Rachel's Tomb. These men would tell him that the donkeys had been found and that his father was worried about him.

As he traveled further, he would come to the Plain of Tabor, and there he would meet three men going to Bethel to make a sacrifice. One of them would have three goats, another three loaves of bread, and the third a bottle of wine. The men would greet him and offer him two loaves of bread. He was to accept them as provision for his journey.

Then, when he would come to a certain hill known as *"the hill of God,"* he would see the camp of the enemy, the Philistines. He was to go on. No harm would come to him.

As he got closer to the city, he would meet a group of prophets coming down from the high place. They would be bearing musical instruments, and they would worship, playing their instruments, singing and prophesying. In Old Testament times, worship, music and the prophetic went hand in hand. These particular prophets were probably from the school of the prophets that Samuel himself had established. But the thing Samuel said would come to pass next was most startling:

> *And the Spirit of the Lord will come upon thee, and thou shalt prophesy with them, and shalt be turned into another man.*   1 Samuel 10:6

Until that moment, there is no record of Saul ever prophesying. It happened by the Spirit of the Lord, and when it happened, his heart was changed. He was now *"another man."*

These signs, Samuel had said, would prove that God had called Saul, and that God's word would be established in his life. All the signs happened just as Samuel had said they would. God will always confirm His word and prove Himself to us.

When it had all been laid out there by the prophet Samuel, Saul seemed overwhelmed by the enormity of it. Could it really be true? Would God choose the most unlikely person out of thousands of other possible candidates? The task he was being given seemed impossible. Would any of the tribes or even his own family listen to him, or even acknowledge him as their king, as God had said? Only God could bring this about.

A HEART CHANGE

As he was on his way home, Saul met the group of prophets, just as Samuel had said he would. And, just as

Samuel had said, the spirit of the prophets came upon him, and he also prophesied. Those who knew Saul and heard him boldly prophesying that day were shocked and began to talk among themselves about it. What had happened to Saul? They knew him and his family, and they had never seen him like this before. The news spread very quickly.

Often, the very hardest place to obey God or to be used by Him is at home or around those who know us. Apparently, Saul had never prophesied before, so this was a new, and possibly very scary, experience for him. That day, God took His word and shifted it from Saul's head into his heart, and suddenly he was a new man. This unusual encounter would change him forever.

A PLACE OF SACRIFICE

After this encounter with the prophets, Samuel had instructed Saul that he was to go to Gilgal, the high place, and wait there for seven days. This was a place of worship and sacrifice, within the confines of his own homeland, and Samuel promised to meet him there after the seven days were fulfilled. There, he would offer burnt offerings and sacrifices and then give Saul more detailed instructions about what he should do and when and how he should do it.

In this way, Saul was to separate himself from everyone else and everything else for seven days. It was a test of trust and obedience, but it was much more than that. Saul had a very serious decision to make. God would not force him to accept this call. It was his to accept or reject.

In the days to come, alone there in that high place before God, Saul humbled himself and accepted the call of God upon his life. In that place of sacrifice, something usually had to die to be offered to God. This time, it was Saul who had to die. He had to die to self. This would take him much more time and require much more effort than receiving the calling ever would.

THE PLACE OF THE SERVANT

It's interesting to note that Saul's servant was still with him. Apparently, his heart must also have been changed after seeing the plan of God for Saul. It now seems obvious that it was no accident that this servant was chosen to accompany Saul on this journey. He witnessed much of what happened during those days and must have pondered it all in his heart. If Saul had a purpose and a calling, then the servant also had a purpose and a calling. God had set him in his place to help Saul, and in the years to come, he probably played a much greater role in Saul's life than he had in the past. This servant may well have become Saul's closest friend, one who would constantly uphold him and encourage him in his new position.

GUARDING THE HEART

After the seven days of waiting and the sacrifice, Samuel sent Saul home. Saul's uncle saw him on the way home and stopped him to ask where he had been. Saul told his uncle that they had gone to look for his father's donkeys, but when they couldn't find them, they had decided to ask the prophet Samuel if he could tell them where they might be. His uncle asked what the prophet had said to him, and Saul's response was very wise. "He told me not to worry because the donkeys were found," he said. He didn't mention any of the rest.

In this way, Saul guarded the calling in his heart. It was a very personal experience, and he must share it only when the Lord directed him to do so. He was not like some, who would run out to tell everyone that they would soon become king. He still wasn't sure that he would have his family's approval or that they would even believe him.

Many of the people around us, because they don't understand what God has spoken to us, give us their opinions, and in the process, they (intentionally or unintentionally) discourage us and sow in us doubts regarding our call. God's call must be digested in our spirits without the undue influence of others.

> *God's call must be digested in our spirits without the undue influence of others!*

There are times and seasons for everything, and when God is ready to announce our call to the world, He will. At this point, Samuel had not yet even informed the nation that God had given His approval for them to have a king.

THE PUBLIC ANNOUNCEMENT

Now it was time for that step, and Samuel called the people to gather at Mizpeh, a place known for gathering together the tribes. Samuel reminded the people of how God had brought them out of Egypt and how He had saved them from their adversaries. He rebuked the people for rejecting God in requesting to have a king like other nations. Still, he said, God had answered their plea for a king and had appointed a man among them. The suspense began to mount.

Samuel then told the people to separate into individual families and tribes. I can imagine that the people were lined up before him in order, from the greatest to the least, and Benjamin came last. He then asked the other tribes to step aside so that the tribe of Benjamin could come forward. When the Benjamites stood before him, Samuel called for Saul's grandfather and all of his descendants. Others moved aside, and this family moved forward.

Then the moment of truth had come. "Would Saul, son of Kish, step forward please," Samuel called out, and everyone held their breath. Saul? Could it be possible? He was a good man, he was good looking, he was tall, he was liked by everyone, and he did have a heart for the people. But could he be a king?

We can't be sure how many minutes passed as they all

waited for Saul to step forward and how long it was before they began to realize that he was not even among them. He had not waltzed out arrogantly and pridefully before them, as many would have done. As they scanned the crowd that day, it should have been easy to spot him. He was so tall that he stood out from all the others. But he just wasn't there.

And where was he? This was his moment. This was the reason he had been born, and now he was nowhere to be found. I can imagine that they asked his parents, his siblings, and his friends. Where was Saul? No one seemed to know.

Finally, Samuel asked the Lord where Saul had gone, and the Lord revealed that the lad had hidden himself *"among the stuff,"* or among their baggage (1 Samuel 10:22). Someone was sent to search for Saul, and, sure enough, that's where they found him.

As Saul was brought forward to face the people, I wonder what he was feeling. These were the people he would serve, but what did he know about serving them? No doubt he was terrified, realizing that he was simply not up to this task (in his own strength).

THE SHOCKING CHOICE

Samuel introduced Saul to the people, saying that God had chosen him to be their king, and that there was *"none like him among all the people"* (1 Samuel 10:24). For sure, Saul was physically taller than all the rest, but he didn't appear to be exceptional or a mighty man of valor, as he stood trembling before the people.

The people were probably shocked by this choice. If they had been given the option of choosing their own king, surely Saul would never have been considered. Even his family, those who knew him best, must have wondered if he was capable of serving in this capacity. After all, to them, he was just Saul. They knew all of his imperfections.

> *When one member of a family is called, the whole family is called!*

Then something wonderful happened. If God had declared through their respected prophet that this was to be their king, then God must know what He was doing. If He saw something in Saul that they had not yet been able to see, then so be it. They had asked God for a king, and God had given them a king. It was a new day. Suddenly, a great cheer went up from the entire crowd:

And all the people shouted, and said, God save the king. 1 Samuel 10:24

What a miracle! The man God chose was well received, despite his own apparent weaknesses.

After Samuel had talked to the people, he sent them all home, including Saul. Amazingly, after the dramatic declaration before all the people, the new king went back to his fields and back to his father's herds.

AN ENTIRE FAMILY CALLED

Before we continue, it's important to note the impact the call of God upon a given individual can have on an entire family. Before Samuel called for Saul that day, he called forth his whole family. There may be some truth to the idea that this was a cultural thing. A son could not be honored without first honoring the entire family, but there was more to it than that. In effect, when one member of a family is called, the whole family is called.

Whether the other members of the family were for Saul or against him didn't matter. They were very much a part of what was happening with him, and it would have both a temporal and an eternal influence on their lives too. This family would never be the same again.

WHERE WAS THE PALACE?

Becoming king, no doubt, seemed like a very exciting prospect. Aren't kings rich and powerful people? There would be plenty of honor connected with the post, and Saul would forever be remembered in history. Surely the people would build him a palace and set him on a throne. It may have all seemed very appealing.

But Saul had already had a change of heart, and we noticed how he stood in humility and fear before God regarding his call. After all, he had just spent seven days at the high place dying to self. He knew that if God didn't

THE RESTLESSNESS OF THE CALL

do this thing, directing his every step, he would surely fail. He had to be totally dependant upon the Lord for strength and wisdom. He had to believe what God had already said to him and trust that He would do it. He had to walk in obedience to His calling.

After all, this was no small thing he was being asked to do. He did not know how to be a king, and since there had never been a king in Israel, he had no precedents to follow, no footsteps to walk in. He would have to relinquish control of his life, his mind, his heart, and his words, and let God do the work for him.

Although the Scriptures do not say so specifically, Saul was probably anointed a second time as he stood before the people that day. Samuel then sealed the entire procedure by writing the details of it in a book and laying it before the Lord. Now His words were established. This prophetic act would be a witness to the fact that God always proves Himself and His word. An important piece of history was written that day.

THE RESTLESS WAITING

Still, the people were not instructed to build a palace or to do anything different. They were to return to their normal duties and way of life, and Saul did the same. This doesn't seem to make sense in our human way of thinking. The people probably wondered when Saul would start acting like the king. Shouldn't he be doing something in his new position?

This is a very dangerous time, when we know what

we're called to do, but we've not yet been set into that office. This is often when restlessness takes over.

Let's face it. Waiting isn't easy. It's not easy for any-body, and it's not easy anytime. We all get tired of waiting, and while we're waiting, what we're waiting for doesn't seem to be a reality.

Will it ever happen? Will our dreams ever come true? Restlessness often causes us to move out before the Lord has given the order. We do it out of fear that nothing will ever happen if we just sit and wait. This is a tragedy, for moving too quickly and, thus, outside of God's plan, will cause us unnecessary trouble and heartache.

THOSE WHO WERE FOR SAUL

The Scriptures speak of a band of men whose hearts God had touched that day, and they chose to accompany Saul to his home. They were convinced that he was God's man, and they would cast their lot with him, come what may.

These were men whom God had also appointed, and they were inspired by the announcement of the prophet. Their hearts were being prepared for service, and they would probably become Saul's ministers, leaders in his government. They would encourage him and lend him their strength and support in the task ahead.

Saul did not choose these men himself. Things were being set up for him by God. He was arranging things so that Saul would not stand alone. These men would not all think exactly alike. God always places very different giftings and anointings together to give strength to the whole group, in order to fulfill His plan.

This need for variety was foreshadowed in the makeup of the sacred oil used in Bible times for anointing. It was not made up of just one substance; it was a mixture of many different substances. It was the proper blending of them all together that provided the beautiful fragrance and great power of the anointing oil. When a group of people all have the same vision, all have a heart connection with God's plan, and all walk in unity, much can be accomplished, even though the individuals that make up that group may be very different from one another.

THOSE WHO WERE AGAINST SAUL

There was another group of people, called in the Bible *"the children of Belial"* (1 Samuel 10:27), who were jealous of Saul and actually despised him. They declared that he was not capable of saving them from their enemies, and, in this way, they showed a lack of respect for Samuel and for the Lord Himself. Theirs was a rebellious spirit, and they refused to give honor to Saul or to bring gifts to him as the others now did. Saul, who had not chosen this position, held his peace when he heard what these men had said. He could easily have tried to prove himself before them, but he left that to God.

It can be very discouraging when others refuse to acknowledge (and actually come against) God's plan for our lives. But we cannot afford to simply write off such people. If we're called to lead one, then we're called to lead all. Those who oppose us may become a serious distraction and cause others to take their eyes off of what God has told them to do, but as the called one, we know what God has said. Therefore we must forgive the others, receive God's healing balm for our own wounds, and insist on focusing on the Lord.

Rather than destroy us, those who oppose us should provoke us to greatness. If our leadership stands the test of time, they may one day jump on the band wagon. In the meantime, we must be determined to fulfill the call, whatever others do.

> *We cannot afford to simply write off those who reject our calling!*

AN ENEMY THREAT

Then, very suddenly, the nation was plunged into crisis. An enemy, Nahash the Ammonite, came against the men of Jabesh, an Israelite family, and threatened to kill them and take their land. The men of Jabesh begged their enemy to make them slaves rather than kill them outrightly. If they did this, the enemy leader said, they would still torment them by putting out their eyes and, in this way, make a mockery of all Israel.

The family asked the enemy for seven days to see what support they could receive from other parts of

Israel. If no one came to their aid in that time, they would willingly submit to the Ammonites.

The Ammonites apparently knew they could easily take this family, but they seemed to enjoy making a game of it. They granted the men of Jabesh the seven days they requested to get together some kind of army for a more challenging fight.

The men of Jabesh felt powerless against this enemy. Their family did not have the strength to stand alone. They needed help. So next, the elders of Jabesh sent out a desperate plea for help to all corners of the nation. Word reached Gibeah, where Saul lived, and when the people heard what was happening, they began to weep.

There was little time to lose, but the Israelites who received this tragic news felt helpless to save their brothers. They didn't see how they could win such a battle, and fear and hopelessness quickly set in.

Saul's Calling Kicked In

When this message arrived in Gibeah, Saul was out in the fields herding animals. It was only when he had come in from the field that he heard the people weeping in hopelessness and asked someone what was wrong. When told about the enemy's threat, Saul was suddenly filled with righteous indignation. The Spirit of the Lord came upon him, and he suddenly knew just what must be done.

Calling for a yoke of oxen, Saul killed them, cut them into pieces, and then had these pieces carried to every corner of Israel. Any man who did not answer this call for help, his message went out, would have his oxen cut in pieces as these had been. Together, he and Samuel would raise an army to rescue their brothers, and anyone who did not join it would be in trouble with him. This message had a chilling effect:

> *And the fear of the Lord fell on the people, and they came out with one consent.* 1 Samuel 11:7

Suddenly, it was as though the anointing of his calling exploded in Saul's spirit. His calling, to protect the inheritance of God's people and their land, so stirred within him that boldness now came over him, and he was able to take control of the situation. This is the same man who had hid the day Samuel announced to the people that he was the one appointed by God to be their king.

It's interesting that when this latest dreadful news came, no one even thought of running to the field to tell Saul. He had to notice their distress when he got in from his work and then ask them what was wrong. Their hopeless weeping showed that they didn't think he could do anything to change the situation. No one had bothered to tell him about it, and no one had encouraged him to do anything about it. But God was speaking to Saul, and He was saying, "Now! This is your time!"

We have come to call what God did in that moment the suddenlies of God. Many times some event or situation will spur our calling. There are times and seasons for

Continued on page 47

PROPHETIC SYMBOLS (1 SAMUEL 9-11)

In the story of Saul, the number three is used over and over again as a prophetic sign regarding his calling. The spiritual meaning of the number three is divine completion, and divine completion always means that a certain matter is established. The Godhead, the three in one, is an example of this truth. Another example is that Jesus rose from the grave after three days, when the plan of salvation was completed.

Multiples of the number three—thirty, three hundred, three thousand, etc.—only intensify the message. Note the following analysis of the number three in Saul's story:

PREPARATION FOR THE APPOINTMENT:
- THREE days were spent searching for his father's donkeys, and it was after THREE days that Saul encountered the prophet Samuel (1 Samuel 9:20).
- THIRTY people were called to the feast which honored Saul (1 Samuel 9:22). Samuel performed other prophetic acts at this feast regarding Saul's call and leading up to his personal anointing. He set Saul in the place of honor, and had Saul served the shoulder of the meat (normally reserved for the priests) (1 Samuel 9:23-24).

THREE SIGNS (1 SAMUEL 10:3-4):
On his way home, Samuel told Saul he would see certain things that would be signs to prove that God was speaking to him.

Some of them were the following:
- THREE men would be traveling together going to Bethel, and they would greet him.

    One of these men would be carrying THREE young goats for a sacrifice.

    Another of them would be carrying THREE loaves of bread. Two of these would be offered to him, and he was to accept them. Bread represents covenant and life. Jesus said that He was *"the Bread of Life"* (John 6:35 and 48).

    A THIRD man would be carrying a bottle of wine. Wine represents the Holy Spirit. Jesus used bread and wine as symbols of His life at the Last Supper with His disciples, setting for us an example, an act of remembrance and communion with God (Luke 22:19-20).

THE VOLUNTEER ARMY THAT RESPONDED TO SAUL'S COMMAND:
- There were THREE hundred thousand men from Israel (1 Samuel 11:8).
- There were THIRTY thousand men from Judah (1 Samuel 11:8).
- Saul divided the army into THREE companies (1 Samuel 11:11).

THREE SIGNIFICANT MEALS:
- A special feast was prepared for Saul's appointment (1 Samuel 9:23).

- Saul was given two loaves of bread for his provision while traveling (1 Samuel 10:4).
- When Saul was established as king, after making sacrifices to God, everyone rejoiced and then ate together (implied in 1 Samuel 11:15). They also ate after their sacrifices in 1 Samuel 9:13 and 19.

THREE SACRIFICES:
- The first sacrifice was at the appointment, when Samuel took Saul to the feast at the high place (1 Samuel 9:19).
- Next, Saul was instructed to wait in Gilgal seven days for Samuel to come there and sacrifice (1 Samuel 10:8).
- The third sacrifice was made when the kingdom was renewed and the position of king was established (1 Samuel 11:15).

THREE PHYSICAL ANOINTINGS FOR SAUL:
- The first anointing occurred at the appointment, the personal calling of Saul (1 Samuel 10:1).
- The second anointing occurred before the whole nation (implied in 1 Samuel 10:24).
- The third anointing occurred before God at the victory sacrifice, when Saul was publicly established as the King of Israel (implied in 1 Samuel 11:15).

different levels of the calling, and this was clearly time for a new season with Saul. God had prepared his heart and had then set him up and given him authority with the people. As for Saul himself, he had already accepted the call, but now he had to make a decision about stepping into it or not. Suddenly, it was time, and just as suddenly, Saul stepped up to the plate.

UNIFIED POWER

The fear of the Lord came upon the people when they received Saul's message, and they responded immediately and in very large numbers. When the volunteers had met in a place called Bezek, they were numbered. Those from Israel numbered three hundred thousand, and those from Judah numbered thirty thousand.

Messengers were then sent to the men of Jabesh to tell them that by the following day (their last day of opportunity), an army would be there to help them. Hearing this, the men of Jabesh were relieved, and their hope was restored. They sent word to their enemies that their seven days would be up the next day, and they could do what they wanted with them at that time. The enemies, as yet, seemed to have no idea that help was on the way.

Saul made the decision to divide his men into three companies and to march on the enemy camp early the next morning. They surrounded their enemies in the pre-dawn darkness, and by midday, most of the Ammonites lay dead on the battlefield. The few who remained were scattered and confused, hardly knowing what had happened to them. Thus, the battle was won easily by the Israelites, and Saul had gained a significant victory.

This was a turning point for God's people. They were no longer losers, and they had a powerful leader. Saul had employed a strategy given to him by God, and it had worked only too well. As he began walking in his calling, the people he was called to serve were saved and set free from their enemies. Fear and hopelessness were removed from them. And God was again glorified in Israel. He had kept His word and proven Himself strong to them that day.

Everything had turned around in a very short space of time!

A TIME TO CELEBRATE

As the victory celebration began in earnest, some of the people wanted Samuel to take the men who had been critical of Saul and refused to accept him as their king and put them to death. Saul replied that no one would die among them that day. This was a day for celebration, not revenge. The Lord had saved Israel from her enemies.

At this moment, Saul clearly had power with the people, and yet he refused to use that power to retaliate against those who had rejected him personally. He was a forgiving man. He was also a humble man. As the celebration continued, he refused to take credit for the victory. God was responsible, not any man.

THE KINGDOM RENEWED AT THE PLACE OF SACRIFICE

Then, Samuel told the people to go to Gilgal. They had something very important to do there. In that place, they would join together in renewing the kingdom. Saul would be formerly made king before them and before the Lord.

During the ceremonies that ensued, Saul was probably anointed again, for the third time. Sacrifices were made and honor was given to the Lord. Everyone rejoiced. God had proven Himself and His word to His people.

Saul now stepped fully into his purpose, fulfilling the call to become King of Israel. He was accepted by the people, and they rededicated themselves to the Lord. Everything had turned around in a very short space of time, and his call (and, thus, his authority) was firmly established before God and also before the people.

Remember that Gilgal was the high place where Saul had first been instructed to go to prepare himself for the call. Now he went back there, accompanied by all the people, to give honor to God for fulfilling and establishing His word and placing a seal of approval upon his leadership. For him and all of Israel, it was a new beginning, a new day.

A GREAT FUTURE PLANNED

As king, Saul honored the Lord and led the Israelites with the close cooperation and oversight of the prophet Samuel. In the days to come, great victories were won, [12] and God proved Himself to His people over and over again. His word had been miraculously fulfilled upon Saul. From tending to his father's animals in the field, he had become a mighty man of God and was now blessed and highly favored. God's hand was upon him, and his future looked very bright indeed. But something happened to change all that.

LOSING SIGHT OF THE CALL[13]

A STRONG KINGDOM

For a time, things went well for King Saul. He became very strong, and his army won many battles.[14] He was able to take for himself the strongest and most valiant men of the kingdom.[15] Then, it appears, this man who had begun so well started to rely upon his own strength and ability and was no longer nearly as dependant upon God. This eventually led to his disobedience.

KING SAUL'S DISOBEDIENCE

One day Samuel again instructed Saul to meet him at the altar at Gilgal, where he would make a sacrifice. Saul went there as before, but after waiting for a while, he became impatient and decided that he had waited for Samuel long enough. He was king. Why did he always have to depend upon Samuel for the sacrifice? He could do it himself. But it was never Saul's place to act as priest, and therefore, in doing this, he was taking upon himself an authority that was not rightfully his.

Not long after Saul had finished making his sacrifice, Samuel arrived. He was very upset when he saw what had happened, and he scolded Saul for not keeping the commandment of the Lord. "God called you," he told Saul, "because you were a man after His own heart, but now it seems obvious that you have changed."

Saul had his excuses for doing what he had done, but Samuel could not accept them. "If you had remained humble before God," he told Saul, "your kingdom would have lasted forever. Now it will not. Your time as king is limited" (1 Samuel 13:13-14, my paraphrase).

When Saul had first received his call, he had gone to the altar at Gilgal and died to himself.[16] He had also honored the Lord at the altar when the kingdom was established.[17] This time was different. He was giving a sacrifice to God, but he was doing it out of a heart of pride and rebellion. In defying Samuel, Saul was defying God Himself. He was no longer a humble man. He had exalted himself. He had begun to depend upon his own strength and power and the use of his own authority, and he was forgetting where it all came from. What a sad day that was!

KING SAUL'S FAILURE

Not long after that, Samuel gave King Saul some more instructions from the Lord. He wanted the Amalekites,

Israel's traditional enemies, to be completely destroyed—both the people and their possessions. Until then, Saul had been very successful in battles against his enemies, but each time he had done things in conjunction with God's prophet and according to God's instructions. This time, he took things into his own hands.

He spared the enemy king, hoping to parade him through the streets and, in this way, gain greater glory for himself and further humiliate his enemy. He also saved the best cattle, oxen, and sheep. He later claimed that it was all to make a greater sacrifice to God, but Samuel did not accept that excuse.

When they next met after this battle, Saul told the prophet that he had successfully completed his assignment to destroy Amalek. This was a lie, since he had only partially obeyed God's instructions. Samuel was not impressed. God had already spoken to him that Saul had disobeyed and that this disobedience was so severe that He could not overlook it. God was sorry He had made Saul king. This news so grieved Samuel that he wept and prayed all night long.

"You have successfully completed your mission, have you?" Samuel asked now. "Then how can you explain the lowing of oxen I hear and the bleating of sheep?"

When faced with his lies, Saul tried to blame *"the people."* They had insisted on sparing these animals, he said, when, in reality, he was the one who had allowed it. He had known exactly what God wanted done, but he had done exactly what he wanted to do. Now his rebelliousness and disobedience was complicated by the fact that he refused to take responsibility for his actions and repent.

Saul and Samuel argued back and forth, Samuel pointing out his failures, and Saul refusing to admit that he had done anything wrong. Finally, it was enough. "This day God has rejected you as king over His people!" Samuel announced. "You're out."

That startling revelation seemed to move Saul, and he suddenly confessed his sin and begged for forgiveness. He was guilty, he said, of listening to *"the people"* and doing what they wanted. That, of course, was just another lie, and Samuel saw through it.

Saul now pleaded with Samuel to go with him to the altar so that he could worship the Lord and find forgiveness. Samuel refused. Saul only wanted to save his power. He was not sincerely seeking God's forgiveness.

At this point, Samuel turned to go. In desperation, Saul grabbed hold of the hem of Samuel's gown, trying to restrain him. The garment tore. "This, too, is symbolic," Samuel told

> *Saul's rebelliousness and disobedience was complicated by the fact that he refused to take responsibility for his actions and repent!*

him. "In the same way you have torn my gown, the Lord has torn the kingdom from your hands. He is giving it to one of your neighbors, a man who is better than you" (1 Samuel 15:28, my paraphrase).

How could Samuel, a man of God since childhood, have been so cold? It was because Saul showed no true repentance. His only fear was losing the kingdom and being punished by God.

KING SAUL'S REQUEST TO BE HONORED

Saul, not wanting his reputation to be destroyed, asked if it were possible that he be honored before the people, as had been done at the time of the sacrifice. Samuel declined to honor this request. For the sake of the kingdom and because he loved Saul, he allowed him to participate in the sacrifice one final time, but that was all.

Saul had failed in his commission to kill the king of the enemy Amalekites, so now Samuel asked that the king be brought to him. There, at the altar at Bethel, Samuel took a sword and completed the task Saul had failed to accomplish. After that act, the two men parted ways, and Samuel never went to see the king again.

SAMUEL'S HURT

Samuel was deeply hurt and grieved that his co-worker and beloved friend in the ministry had failed. They had shared the same vision. He had taken no joy in delivering God's harsh message to Saul. For him, this was not a cause for rejoicing, but for grief. He was disappointed and grieved his loss, and in the coming days, he felt lonely and rejected himself.[18]

In all of this, Samuel appears to have had very little compassion, and his words seem very harsh, but keep in mind that he was in a most difficult situation. Many of the people of that day might not have understood his words and actions.

King Saul had become very popular with the people. He had made them strong and won many battles for them, and so they loved him. It would not be easy for them to understand Samuel's position. As always, the problem was that they only saw the outward appearance, when God saw the heart.

In the days to come, Samuel, appointed by God as prophet for that particular time, would need healing for his emotions. Any man, great or small, would have suffered emotionally from such a tragedy.

A Sad Ending

When the time came for Samuel to anoint another man to be king and David was chosen, Samuel feared that Saul would kill him.[19] Because of this, David was secretly anointed, but that didn't matter. The moment David was anointed in Saul's place, the kingly anointing lifted from Saul and came to rest on David.[20] In the coming days, Saul became miserable and depressed.[21] He still remained in his position as king, and, as king, he fought other battles.[22] In the meantime, David, as his successor, was being prepared and set up for his calling.

On several occasions, Saul tried to kill David. He was jealous of his anointing and blamed him for his own troubles.[23] Just before his death, Saul went so far as to disguise himself and seek counsel from a witch, something he had previously outlawed for the people.[24] How ironic it is that the life of Saul, who was called to protect God's people and their land from the enemy, was ended, along with the life of his sons, in battle against the enemy.[25]

We all love stories with happy endings, but unfortunately, Saul's story did not end as it should have. It was not God's plan that failed; Saul's pride and rebellious spirit caused him to fail in his position. Instead of displaying true repentance and seeking forgiveness, he insisted on blaming others. As a result, he lost his spiritual insight.

God does promise to restore us the moment He sees true repentance in our hearts, but what does He do in the meantime? The position we have been filling often cannot wait for us. Since we're not filling it properly, someone else must do it. Saul's time on the throne was finished, and it was David's turn.

God's call had never left Saul, but God's anointing had definitely lifted from him. This left him in misery. If he had truly repented at the altar of God, this could all have been avoided. What a sad story! Let it not be yours.

CHAPTER 2

DAVID

Now therefore so shalt thou say unto my servant David, Thus saith the LORD of hosts, I took thee from the sheepcote, from following the sheep, to be ruler over my people, over Israel.   2 Samuel 7:8

As we saw in Chapter 1, Saul was anointed by the prophet Samuel to be the first king over Israel. He had a heart after the Lord, and all went well for him at first. His call was to be captain over God's people and to protect them and their land from any and all enemies. Then, after he had become successful and beloved of the people, Saul's heart changed. He became rebellious and disobedient to the Lord and to His prophet. When Saul refused to repent, God removed His anointing from him and placed it upon David. Now this lad, a mere shepherd boy, would become the next king.[1]

CHOSEN BY GOD[2]

THE APPOINTMENT

One day, while Saul was still sitting as king, God spoke to Samuel and told him that He had chosen one of the sons of a man named Jesse to be the next king of Israel. He should, therefore, go and anoint this man with oil. Samuel was afraid that King Saul might kill him if he learned that he was about to anoint someone else to be king, so he asked the Lord what he should do. The Lord instructed him to take a calf and go to sacrifice, and then invite Jesse and his sons to sacrifice with him.

Jesse, the Bethlehamite, had eight sons, and God didn't tell Samuel which one of them He intended to make king. He was only told to go. While he was there with them, the Lord would speak to him and show him which son to anoint. Samuel went on his way to Bethlehem, trusting that God would do exactly what He had said.

When Samuel arrived at Bethlehem, the leaders of the city were afraid and asked if his mission was peaceful. He told them he had come to sacrifice unto the Lord, and wanted to invite Jesse and his sons to sanctify themselves and sacrifice with him. Only seven of the sons were present at first; the youngest was left in the fields watching the sheep.

At the sacrifice, Samuel had each of Jesse's sons pass before him, as he sought God to see which one He would appoint. When the first son, Eliab, passed by, Samuel thought for sure he must be the one. He was older and, perhaps, taller than the others, and he just looked like the leader in the group. But the Lord said he was not the one. Outward appearance did not concern Him, the Lord said. This was a matter of the heart.

SAMUEL WAS PUZZLED

After each of the seven sons had passed before him and God had said no to them all, Samuel was puzzled. He knew God had sent him. What was he to do now? He asked Jesse if there were any more sons. Jesse said there was one more, but he has just "a kid." Nevertheless, Samuel asked if this youngest son, David, could be brought in as soon as possible. He must pass before him as the other sons had.

Samuel showed his human side that day when he took it for granted that the oldest of the sons would be the chosen leader. Being the oldest, he must have acted personable and confident, and apparently he was a good communicator.

> *Outward appearance did not concern the Lord! This was a matter of the heart!*

If Eliab was tall and handsome, he might well have reminded Samuel of King Saul. He just looked like kingly material. David, on the other hand, was the least likely of the sons to be considered. His father had not even given him a passing thought, very possibly because of his age and his lack of experience. Until then, his only duties had been tending the sheep. The older sons had more proven skills and abilities.

THE FIRST ANOINTING

When David came in, the prophet noticed that he had reddish cheeks, and he cut a very striking figure. But there was more. The moment he saw David, the Lord spoke to Samuel that this was the chosen one. Immediately and without hesitation, the prophet took the horn of oil he had brought for the purpose and anointed the lad in front of his father and his brothers.

In that moment, the Spirit of the Lord came upon David, and it would remain upon him in this special way. This physical anointing would mark the beginning of David's appointed call. The anointing he received that day would give him inner strength for the training and preparation he must undergo for his future position.

As we have seen, the call is very personal. Each one must either accept or reject it. David's pure heart before the Lord insured his acceptance of this call.

DAVID'S BROTHERS MUST HAVE BEEN SHOCKED

In the meantime, Jesse and his family were shocked that their little David was being anointed to become the next king. It's very possible that one or more of the brothers, thinking that *he* was much more qualified for this post, could have become very angry with this turn of events.

Why shouldn't they be confused and angry? There was nothing to show that David was in any way qualified to be a king. This seemed impossible to them. But God, seeing the hearts of all, had set His desires upon David, and He Himself would prepare and qualify the lad for this seemingly impossible call. Even before the day David officially took office, in fact, from this very moment and forward, everything that David touched would be blessed.

Because of the circumstances, this was a very private ceremony. There was no announcement to the nation, and no one rolled out the red carpet for David that day. He also did not assume the throne immediately. The position was not open. Saul still sat on the throne, and if word got out to him about this little ceremony, he would be very angry. He, his advisors, and his military leaders would feel threatened by David and might decide to do him harm.

It would have been especially offensive to Saul that it was David who was chosen. David was a much younger man (too young), he had no preparation for the job (too little preparation), and he had very little experience (too little experience). Yet God said this was the one, and he was anointed for the job.

Then, without further fanfare, Samuel went home, and David went back to the fields to tend to his sheep. Nothing seemed to have changed. Or did it? In one sense, nothing had changed, but in another very real sense, everything had changed. Now, while he was waiting for his call to unfold, David had renewed purpose and much to ponder in his heart. He now had his eye on a specific goal that he could work toward.

PREPARATIONS AT HOME

Even David's time spent in the field, keeping his father's sheep, would prove to be a time of preparation for his call. It had already helped him to develop the pure servant's heart. There, on the hillsides, he became very skilled on the harp because he used it extensively to worship the Lord. As a worshiper, David communed with God and developed a strong relationship with Him. This would make him a far better king.

> *As a worshiper, David communed with God and developed a strong relationship with Him!*

While tending the sheep, David also became very skilled with the sling shot. He practiced with it often, so that, if need be, he could drive off any animals attempting to prey on the flocks. These sheep had been entrusted to his care, and he must protect them at all costs. In all of this, he trusted God and was confident of His protection, and, when the time came, this proved vital. With God's help, he was able to kill the wild animals that dared to attack his flock.

David took his responsibility seriously and wasn't lazy about it, even though he had plenty of spare time to spend as he watched over the sheep. He was known as a young person of good behavior and sound judgment. Very young in life he became a person of excellence, and the skills that he developed though his disciplined life in the fields were exceptional and would become part of his ministry, as doors were opened to him in the future.

PURPOSEFUL WAITING (THE TRAINING PERIOD)[3]

CHOSEN FOR A POSITION IN THE PALACE

The moment David was anointed to be king, there was a transference of anointing from King Saul to him. Saul was not yet aware of the fact that the anointing for king now rested on David, but he was very much aware that the Spirit of the Lord had departed from him. He was now troubled and depressed, moody and angry.

Saul's servants, concerned for his welfare and that of the nation, suggested that he allow them to seek out a person skilled in playing the harp, a person who could play before him and calm his frazzled nerves. Saul agreed to this request.

Someone in the palace had heard of the unusual skills of David, and they suggested that he be called. He had, they said, a reputation as a valiant person who behaved himself well. He should have no difficulty performing before the king.

The most important point made that day was that David was anointed by God. Because of this, he would be able to combat the demons that tormented Saul and to bring him peace. It was a high recommendation, and it proves that David didn't have to tell people that God's hand was on him. The anointing upon his life spoke for itself.

It all sounded good to Saul, so he sent messengers to Jesse, asking if he would be willing to send his son to interview for the job. Jesse was only too happy to comply. He sent David, and with him, he sent the king a gift consisting of bread, wine, and a young goat. David auditioned before King Saul, and the king instantly loved him.

The Lord had clearly set up this situation for David, but King Saul probably saw himself in the lad (because of the spirit he had carried in the past). The king sent word to Jesse, asking that David be allowed to stay with him and become his armor bearer.

This was a great honor, for the king always required the best servants in every position, but David was far more than an armor bearer to Saul. When an evil spirit would vex and upset the king, David would take his harp and play until it departed. There was such an anointing upon him that when he played, the presence of the Lord would fill the room. Every time it happened, only peace remained.

In the back of their minds, Jesse and David were probably both wondering if this was the way in which David would become king. Being hired to work in the palace as a personal servant to the king could only bring him closer to the position, when it finally did become vacant. In the end, it was not to be the opportunity it seemed to be, but at least David was now learning the protocol of the palace and the ways of government. This, too, would be an important training ground for his future position.

THREATS FROM THE ENEMY

Then, the Philistines gathered to fight against Israel, and Saul and his men were forced to go out against them. The Philistines encamped on a certain hill, and the Israelites decided to encamp on the opposite hill, with only a valley separating them. From there, they would survey their prospects and decide on the proper action to take. But things did not go well for them.

The Philistines had a man they called their champion. He was a giant of a man named Goliath. Every day Goliath stood on the hill in full view of the Israelites and taunted them, demanding that they send some brave soldier out to fight him personally. If he lost, he said, the Philistines would then serve their Israelite neighbors, but if he won, the Israelite soldiers would all become slaves of the Philistines.

Goliath's huge stature, his very intimidating armor and weaponry, and his threats brought great fear to King Saul and to his army. Saul was clearly not the man he had been when he called the nation to war against the Ammonites. He now sought among his men for someone bold enough to go out and fight against Goliath, but he found none.

David Was Sent Back Home

Jesse's three oldest sons had gone to battle with King Saul, and so David, being the youngest and least experienced of them all, was now called home to tend the sheep. He was not there to see this giant of a man threatening and bullying into submission the armies of Israel.

Goliath presented himself each day for forty days with continued threats to the Israelites, and they felt helpless to respond. They were sure that they could not win against this giant. It was an impossible situation. All hope was drained from them as each day they were sent a little deeper into their pit of despair.

Then one day David's father told him to take some food to his brothers and their captain at the battle front and to bring back a report of how things were going. This could not have come at a more opportune time. Having concluded their days of torment and humiliation, the Philistines had finally formed ranks and were moving out toward the Israelite camp. In response, the Israelite soldiers were moving out to meet them, but the mood was glum. No one expected victory.

David left the sheep with a keeper and very early in the morning left to do his father's bidding. When he arrived at the front, he saw his fellow Israelites preparing to go into the valley to fight the enemy army. He left his carriage and ran to find his brothers among them.

David's Introduction to Goliath

He found them and gave them the provisions he had brought, but then, as he was talking with them about how things stood with the Philistines, Goliath came out shouting as before. David could not believe what he was seeing. Grown men, the bravest of the brave among the ranks of Israel, now ran with terror. The Philistines would not have to defeat the Israelites in battle. They were already overcome by fear.

In time, the giant tired of his antics and drew back, and as the men began to breath again and then talk among themselves, Goliath was the topic of every conversation. David quickly learned that a great reward was being offered to any man who would be willing to fight Goliath and kill him.

> *David could not believe what he was seeing!*

Saul desperately needed this reproach and disgrace to be removed from his camp. If not, how could he and his men ever face their families again? Or would they live to face anyone? Still, despite the offer of riches, a tax-free future for his family, and the hand of the king's daughter in marriage, no man had yet stepped forward to accept the challenge.

David was shocked by the reaction of these men. This giant, he told them, was a pagan, an infidel, an unbeliever. He was living outside the covenant. How could such a man, however large he was, be permitted to disgrace the armies of the living God? David had such confidence in God that he couldn't understand how the men could let such a challenge stand.

ELIAB'S SCORN

Eliab, David's oldest brother, overheard David talking to the men, trying to encourage them to regain their faith and trust in God, and it made him very angry. He didn't need to have his failure pointed out by his kid brother.

Who was this kid to be advising them all? He had no experience in war, and he had not been there in this situation to understand why they were reacting the way they were. Without mercy, he cut David down in front of the others, suggesting, in no uncertain terms, that he had only come there out of pride and to get attention. His advice, such as it was, was of very little value because all he knew was how to attend to a few sheep. Why didn't he just go back to those sheep now?

David's response to Eliab was measured and kind. He had a purpose in what he was doing, he told his older brother. Then he turned and continued his conversation with the men.

But didn't Eliab have a point? David was known for his music, not for being an experienced warrior. And it was true that he had not been there to experience the situation. He'd been back home in the fields.

On the other hand, David had a point. Because he had

been at home in the fields communing with God, as was his custom, the presence and anointing he carried with him gave him strength and confidence.

He was also right about the giant. This man had no right to defy the armies of the living God. He may have been big, but he didn't know God. David saw no reason the Israelite soldiers should fail in battle against such a man.

Because he was so confident in his Source, David didn't back off when his brother tried to humiliate him in front of other soldiers. These, too, were men of God, and they were tired of hearing these constant threats from an infidel. They were tired of being beaten down, feeling hopeless, and not knowing what to do. David had come into the camp as an outsider, almost like an evangelist, fresh and fired up, trying to renew their hope, and his message was hitting home.

TAKING A STAND AGAINST THE ENEMY

Word got to King Saul about what David was saying, and he sent for the lad. David told the king that he and his men should not be afraid of this giant. If they would permit him to, he would go out and fight the big man. The king pointed out David's obvious lacks. He was much too young to fight against such an experienced soldier. David's response was electrifying.

One day, while watching his father's sheep, he had been confronted by a lion intent on spoiling the herd. With God's help, he had fought the lion and killed it.

Then, on another occasion, a bear had attacked. He was all alone, with no one to help him. He called on God to help him, and then he went after the bear. The result was that he'd killed it too. If he could kill a lion and a bear with God's help, who was this Philistine to defy God and His people? God had protected him from the lion and from the bear, and He would also protect him from this giant.

> **David spoke with such courage and confidence that what he said encouraged others!**

Several things about David's presentation were captivating. For one thing, he spoke with such courage and confidence that what he said encouraged others. The fact that he was willing to risk his own life for what he believed in was the clincher. When he had begun this conversation, Saul was probably reluctant to even consider David's proposal. After all, what would it look like for the king to send a lad out to fight his battles? Now, Saul was convinced. If anyone could face this giant, this boy could.

SAUL IDENTIFIED WITH MIRACLES

Saul had experienced God's miracles in the past, so what David was saying was not altogether new to him. It struck some long-dormant chord in his inner being. But could David win? Perhaps it was the desperation of the situation that caused King Saul to give him the chance.

DAVID

The other members of the army were probably shocked at Saul's decision, and it may well have appeared to them as most unwise. Because of this, it is very possible that many refused to stand forth and cheer David on. If so, he would fight this battle alone—as he had others before.

King Saul insisted on outfitting David with his own armor and with a sword, as was customary for any battle of the time. But David, who was not accustomed to armor, told the king he simply couldn't use it. It didn't fit him right, and he wasn't comfortable with it. He preferred to go out in his own way, with his own proven style and the skills God had anointed him with.

David then picked up his shepherd's staff, checked to make sure he had his faithful sling, and headed off in the direction of the giant. On his way, he picked up a few smooth stones from the brook and put them into his shepherd's bag.

Even though he had been given permission to go out to battle in this way, no one expected him to fight like this and win. His style was unorthodox, to say the least, and would surely not have been accepted by military men of the day. In fact, what he was doing probably seemed like a lot of foolishness to the warriors on both sides of the battle.

THE BATTLE WAS WON

When Goliath was informed that he finally had a challenger, he prepared himself and went out to the battlefield with great eagerness. He intended to fight this battle and win. A man chosen to carry his huge shield went before him. When Goliath peered over the shield to see who his enemy was, he was shocked. "Is this a joke?" he asked. There, before him, stood a kid with no visible weapons and no armor.

"Are you trying to make fun of me?" he threatened. Then he cursed David for coming out to fight with a stick rather than a sword. "If you're serious," the giant thundered, "I'll kill you with no effort at all."

But David was not intimidated. "You may have great weapons," he told the giant, "but that's nothing compared to the power of my God, in whose name I now come. Today you will die, your head will be removed, and through it, God will be glorified."

How could David say such things to a man who was so intimidating? He knew the power of the Invisible. He was just a vessel. The battle was the Lord's, and he would prove it that day. In his heart, he had already killed the giant, and through faith, what was in his heart would now become reality.

DAVID'S WORDS ANGERED GOLIATH

Goliath was angered by all this talk and came toward David. Instead of running away, David now ran toward the giant. With great calm, he took his sling in hand, inserted one of the smooth stones, and pulled it back for release. That tiny stone, if it hit the giant in any area protected by his extensive armor, would feel like little more than a gnat. It would bounce off, and Goliath would lunge forward with even greater speed and ferocity.

With a final prayer, David let go of the sling. The rock flew through the air and struck the giant in one of the few vulnerable spots, right in the middle of his forehead. It hit him with such force that he fell to the ground and didn't move.

While the Philistine was thus stunned, David ran forward, drew out the giant's own sword and used it to cut off his head. The great champion of the Philistines was dead.

The Spell Was Broken

Within moments of this accomplishment, the rest of the Philistines suddenly rose up from their places and ran in fear. Then the Israelite army suddenly came alive and ran after the enemy soldiers, overtaking them, and killing them. When the Israelites had finished killing as many of the Philistine soldiers as possible, they set about sacking their tents, gathering up the spoils of battle.

David Was Taken Before Saul

Abner, the captain of the king's host, escorted David, who was holding Goliath's head in his hands, and led him to the king. Saul was impressed and very pleased. A great victory had been won that day because of this lad, and the word that David had proclaimed about Goliath and to Goliath had came true. David didn't do it all himself, but what he had done stirred faith and hope in the rest of the army of God, and they were able to rise up and do what the Lord had commanded them to do.

Even though David was anointed to kill the giant, he had to be careful not to take too much credit for the victory that day. Through faith, he had followed the direction of God.

In order to win, he had been forced to ignore the opinions of the other men. He had no time to win their approval. This was an emergency, and it brought out the best in him. Other tests, like his experiences with the lion and the bear, had prepared him for this day and for the giant. Now, after killing the giant, he knew that if he would be obedient to God, not only could he be victorious in the days to come, but he could also lead many others to victory. It was an important moment in his life.

A Friend Was Appointed

By the time King Saul had finished talking to David that day, the heart of his son Jonathan had been knit to the heart of David. The two of them became best friends. To seal their pact of friendship, Jonathan gave David his own robe, his own sword, and his own bow and belt.

This proved to be a friendship appointed by God. Jonathan, who was the logical choice to become the next king, was not threatened by his close friend's success. He was happy for David and ready to help him in any way he could.

Taken to Another Level

Now King Saul took David on to work with him full-time. David did whatever the king told him to do, and in doing so, showed much wisdom and handled himself well. Without any regard for his age, the king placed him in a leadership position over the men of war. David thus had great favor with the king and with his men, and was respected and accepted by the people and by the king's servants.

Everything seemed to be going so well that David probably wondered to himself if the Lord would not just move him on into the position of king, the position he was called and anointed for. But it didn't happen. It still wasn't the right time. This was just another step in his preparation, and David must continue his training for leadership.

It still wasn't the right time! This was just another step in his preparation!

TRIALS AT HOME

David was victorious in so many of the battles he was sent to fight that the women of Israel danced and sang victory songs lauding his exploits. One song in particular annoyed Saul when he heard it. It stated that Saul had slain his thousands, but David had slain his tens of thousands. This caused Saul to be very jealous of David. It appeared that the people now considered David greater than himself, and that was too much for a proud king to bear.

The next day Saul had one of his troubling episodes, and David was called to play the harp to calm him down. While David was playing, Saul threw a javelin and tried to kill the lad. He did this twice, and David was forced to run out.

Saul was now afraid of David because he knew that the Spirit of the Lord was with him. He himself, King over Israel, no longer carried the anointing, and he was jealous that David did. He decided to demote David. Instead of being over all of the men of war, he would be a captain over only one thousand men. This must have been humiliating for David, and yet he behaved himself wisely and did not develop a rebellious spirit or resent the king. He insisted on respecting him as God's anointed.

Saul continued to plot against David. He now offered the lad his oldest daughter Merab in marriage, if David would go out and fight the Philistines. His hope was that they would kill David. David had already been promised Merab as his wife if he killed the giant, but Saul had conveniently forgotten that promise. Now, Saul took advantage of David again when the lad humbly answered that he felt unworthy to be the son-in-law of the king. Merab was given to another man. From the beginning, David had been lied to and treated unfairly by Saul, and that didn't seem about to change.

Then, Saul's youngest daughter, Michal, fell in love with David, and Saul took advantage of this infatuation to try to trap David again. The dowry for her hand in marriage was set at one hundred foreskins of the Philistines. Saul was sure that David would be killed trying to accumulate this bounty. But, of course, he wasn't. God was with him.

David did eventually became the king's son-in-law by marrying Michal, and, although Saul was unable to win his war against the youth, he never stopped trying. In the process, he became David's chief enemy. But the more Saul came against David, the more it seemed that the people loved the boy. And through all the hurt of this official abuse, David behaved himself wisely and maintained a proper spirit.

After Saul tried to place David in a position in battle where he would surely be killed and it didn't work, he spoke to Jonathan and all his servants openly and suggested that they kill David. But Jonathan loved David. Rather than kill him, he warned David to hide until the next morning. That night he would talk to his father to see if he could save David's life. Saul agreed not to kill him, and David returned to his place in the palace.

Things were okay between them for a short while, but then one day Saul again threw his javelin at David. David escaped. The next morning, Saul sent messengers to watch for him and kill him. This time, it was Michal who told David what her father had done. To save him, she let him down from a window so that he could escape. When Saul learned that David had escaped, he was very angry.

Leaving the Palace

David was now forced to flee for his life, and he went to find the prophet Samuel. Samuel had anointed him.

Maybe he would have an answer for this unusual behavior. David told Samuel all that had happened, including the numerous threats on his life. Together, they went and stayed at the school of the prophets.

Saul had his network of spies, and learning where David was, he sent messengers to bring him back—three different times. Each time, when the messengers arrived at the school of the prophets, they saw the prophets prophesying and Samuel standing before them as their leader. And each time the spirit of the prophets came upon the messengers, and they could only prophesy. In the end, they left without David.

> As much as he loved David, Jonathan could no longer protect him from his father!

Since the others had failed, Saul himself went to get David, and the exact same thing happened to him. In each case, God did not remove the trial; He supernaturally protected David.

David returned to Jonathan again, and Jonathan told him he was sure his father would kill him if he could find him. David hid, while Jonathan tried to determine if there was any hope that his father might change his mind. In a heated discussion between Saul and Jonathan, Saul told his son that as long as David was around, he (Jonathan) would have no chance of ever becoming king. Therefore Saul was determined to kill David.

Jonathan didn't bother to tell his father that he had long ago given up the idea of becoming king himself. He recognized David as Israel's next king. That thought would only have infuriated his father. Jonathan then told David that he should run for his life and never come back as long as Saul was alive and in control. As much as he loved David, Jonathan could no longer protect him from his father.

Before he left, David asked Jonathan to make sure that his family members were not cut off and that they were treated with kindness. Jonathan and David then renewed their vow of friendship, and David departed.

It Didn't Make Sense

What was happening didn't seem to make sense, but David had no choice but to flee to protect his life. He had been not only part of Saul's family; he had also served as one of the nation's important leaders. Now he had to leave his wife, Michal, Saul's daughter, his dearest friend Jonathan, Saul's son, and the rest of his family and close friends. He was also leaving his job and his place of worship.

This must have been perplexing and frustrating. Through no fault of his own, David's entire world had collapsed. Feeling abandoned, hurt, and rejected by his father-in-law, he was forced to leave with just what he could carry on his body, and with no promise of future provision. From that moment on, his life would be in serious danger.

What a sad situation! To David, everything must have seemed hopeless about then. He had been stripped of all that had become important in his life, and now he had to be totally dependant upon God. He must have wondered if he had "messed up" in some way and brought this all upon himself. Could he have possibly understood why all of this was happening? And would the call of God upon his life ever be fulfilled? It seemed further away now than ever before.

THE RESTLESS WAITING[4]

WHERE COULD DAVID GO?

David now went to a place called Nob to see the priest there. He didn't tell the priest what was going on with him, but he asked for some bread and also for the sword of Goliath. Without questioning, the priest gave these to him, and David left. He had some bread, and he had a very big sword. Where could he go now?

David ended up living in a cave. When his parents and siblings discovered where he was, they went to visit him there. He placed his parents in Moab for their protection, and then he wandered from place to place, hiding in forests or caves or any other place that seemed to afford protection. Anytime Saul learned of his whereabouts, he had to move again. This, then, became David's life.

In all, Saul made twenty-one attempts on David's life.

To spite his son-in-law, he now gave Michal to another man to be his wife. That must have added insult to injury.

On one occasion, Jonathan, David's heart-friend, heard where he was hiding and went to encourage him. He reminded David of the word of the Lord that he would become king and assured him that God would fulfill His word.[5] David's heart must have been near to bursting at times with hurts of all kinds. He had to choose whether to forgive and be healed or to become a bitter and angry man.

In time, a group of men, at first numbering some four hundred, allied themselves with David. They were misfits from every corner of society, and, like David, they were on the run. Now they all ran together. Others joined them, until their numbers reached six hundred. This was a small army, and David became their captain.

DAVID HAD NOT ABANDONED HIS FAITH

David had not abandoned his faith. He continually called upon the Lord for help and direction. Could he have possibly understood that what he was experiencing was preparing him to serve better?

Over time, David became very experienced in developing proper strategies and in making quick decisions. He had to promote unity within his diverse and unruly group so that his men could accomplish their day-to-day goals. I have no doubt that he taught these men how to worship, since that was such a big part of his own personal life. In the end, this group of men, who had each come to him with "messed up" lives, became known as *David's mighty men.* When he eventually became king, they would be his trusted servants. They were changed because of the presence of God that David carried upon his life.

OPPORTUNITIES TO KILL SAUL

On two different occasions, David had the opportunity to kill Saul, but he refused to do it. This man was his king, and he had been placed in that position by God Himself. David would not take it upon himself to do the king any harm. Both times, Saul came to know of what had happened, and this must have made him think long and hard. The result was that he retreated and left David alone for awhile.

On several occasions, Saul even acknowledged that David would one day become king.[6] But his bitter spirit would not let him rest, and after a short while, he began hunting his son-in-law again, as though he could somehow alter God's plan.

Because Saul was obsessed with this mission to kill David, he didn't deserve to be spared, and yet David insisted on sparing his life. He would not take matters into his own hands, but he would trust God to take care of him and perform His word. He dared not touch God's anointed, even though his own life was at risk (see 1 Chronicles 16:22).

God continually protected David. The Scriptures

note that no one saw him the night he crept in to take King Saul's spear:

> *So David took the spear and the cruse of water from Saul's bolster; and they gat them away, and no man saw it, nor knew it, neither awaked: for they were all asleep; because a deep sleep from the LORD was fallen upon them.*
>
> 1 Samuel 26:12

As much as he was suffering, David was still God's man, and God was helping him every step of the way.

DAVID WAS FORCED TO LEAVE ISRAEL

Eventually, David and his men and their families were forced to live outside of Israel in an area controlled by the Philistines.[7] They felt less threatened living with their enemies than they did living in their own country. Called to be the king of Israel, David could not even live within the borders of his own land. How sad!

David would not take matters into his own hands, but he would trust God to take care of him and perform His word!

Even in this time of great trial, David did not think only of himself. After winning the battle of Ziklag against the Philistines, he sent gifts from the spoils of battle to show appreciation to various people who had helped him and his men as they ran from Saul.[8]

But this did not mean that David was not distressed. What was going on with his life? Had he misunderstood what God had said? The prophet Samuel had died, so there was no way to ask him to confirm it all again.[9] Years were passing, and things were not changing. Would he ever become king? Or was he doomed to wander forever in this way?

THE DEATH OF SAUL[10]

Then one day, a day that seemed like all other days, King Saul and three of his sons, including Jonathan, died in a battle with the Philistines. When some of the Israelites learned what had happened, they fled from their cities, expecting large areas to now be overrun by the enemy. This was a mistake. The Philistines gladly took advantage of it and gained more territory by taking their people in to inhabit the now-abandoned cities.

BECOMING KING[11]

THE SECOND ANOINTING[12]

Even though Saul had died, there was still a lot of animosity toward David among the king's family members and close staff. David didn't know quite what to do. The Lord told him to move back to Judah, and the elders there lost no time in anointing him to be their king. This was definitely a positive thing, but it was only another step toward his full calling. David was called to be King of all Israel, not just King of Judah. Still, he would remain King of Judah for the next seven years.

THE KINGDOM WAS DIVIDED[13]

Abner, the son of the captain of Saul's host, took it upon himself to make Ishbosheth, one of Saul's remaining sons, king over the rest of Israel, and this resulted in constant strife between the house of Saul and the house of David. For his part, David became stronger and stronger.

Abner and King Ishbosheth also had a lot of strife between the two of them, and in the ensuing power struggle, Abner put out feelers to David, suggesting that he might be willing for all of Israel to be transferred to David's rule. What would David require?

Before he was even willing to talk to Abner, David first required that his wife Michal be returned to him. This was done.

Next, Abner called for a gathering of the people of Israel to put this proposal to them. Before it could go very far, both he and King Ishbosheth were killed, and the agreement was never completed.

THE THIRD ANOINTING (KING OF ISRAEL), THE CALL ESTABLISHED[14]

After King Ishbosheth died, Israel was in dire need of a leader. The elders of Israel met and then went in delegation to David to ask him to become their king. They had not forgotten how he had saved them from the Philistines as a lad and how he had successfully led the military under Saul. More importantly, they said, they knew that the Lord had set him as captain over Israel.

David, of course, had known it all along. Now his time had finally come, and he willingly agreed to be their king. David was then anointed King of all Israel, and Judah reunited with the rest of the country. He moved to Jerusalem and ruled the nation from there for the next thirty-three years.

> *David had known it all along, but now his time had finally come!*

THAT'S HOW IT HAPPENS

And that's how it happens. Everything seems to be delayed by whatever prevailing circumstance, and the ticking of the clock tends to make us believe it will never happen. But if we're faithful, it comes—often suddenly and unexpectedly—and we have to be ready for it. What we experience in the meantime will prepare us for that day.

In a very short span of time, God's word was established upon David. His season had finally come, and all was in order. Despite every impossibility and every obstacle, God had done just what He said He would do.

Thankfully, David had remained faithful and kept his heart pure before the Lord.

The preparation, or training, if you will, had been long and arduous, but now a shepherd boy would become king and leader of God's people. He would enjoy, in the years to come, great favor with both God and man, and much would be accomplished through his life.

It could not have been easy for him to be hated and hunted by the most powerful man in the land, the king himself, and yet God had kept His hand upon David and had supernaturally protected him. Every trial that he faced only drove him to connect more with the heart of God, and he had continued to honor and worship Him through it all. Now, after years of restless waiting and oft shattered hopes and dreams, David was firmly established as King of Israel, as God had planned all along.

THE PROPHECY OF THE CALL FULFILLED

God had brought David from the sheepfold to the throne of Israel.[15] For many years, it had seemed to be common knowledge in Israel that he was called to be the next king. Aside from his own family and the prophet Samuel,[16] King Saul himself knew it,[17] as did Jonathan, his son,[18] the leaders of Israel,[19] and many others exhibited no doubt about this calling. There was constant divine protection over David's life, and the anointing upon him was obvious to all. The fact that God preserved him wherever he went spoke volumes.[20] Then, finally, David, who had long been called to be the king of Israel, actually *became* the king of Israel. After that, David became great[21] and remained king until his death, impacting many generations.

DAVID'S FAILURE[22]

DAVID SINNED

As great as King David was, he was not perfect. He was human and, as a human, he was prone to sin. One day he sent Joab, the leader of his army, out to battle, while he himself remained at home in Jerusalem. After resting for awhile one day, he went up on his rooftop to catch the view of the surrounding area. What he saw there was something he had not counted on, something that would change the course of his life.

As he peered over, he saw a woman bathing on a nearby rooftop. She was very beautiful, and he was suddenly struck with a pang of desire. He wanted this woman.

And why not? He was the king. Who could blame him? he must have reasoned. After all that he had suffered in the years leading up to his rule, was it wrong of him to want a few moments of comfort in the arms of a beautiful woman? Surely not. And who would dare question the king?

Whatever David told himself that day worked. Laying aside all decency and decorum, he sent one of his messengers to have the woman brought to him. Then he made love to her and sent her home.

Some time later, this woman, whom he now knew to

be Bathsheba, wife of Uriah the Hittite (who faithfully served in his army), sent him a message saying that she was pregnant. This was a problem because her husband had been away fighting in the war, and it would be obvious to all that this was not his child.

Until that moment, David may have thought that his sin would not find him out. Now, he knew better, and he became desperate to find some way of resolving this matter before it turned into something even uglier.

An idea came to David. He would call for Uriah to come home, saying it was to deliver him a personal report of how the battle was going. After the report had been given, he would send the Hittite home to sleep for the night before returning to the front. That should take care of the situation.

It seemed like a very good plan and one that should work. What David had not counted on was Uriah's loyalty to his fellow troops. He refused to go home that night and enjoy sleeping in his own bed with his own wife, when his fellow soldiers were out on the battlefield suffering in tents. Instead, he slept near the door of David's house.

Perplexed, David had to go back to the drawing board. He came up with another great idea. He would insist that Uriah remain for a special dinner, and during that dinner, he would fill the man with plenty of good wine. When Uriah was drunk, he would surely want to go home and sleep with his wife. It was a good plan, but again it was foiled, when Uriah, instead of going home, spent the night in the servants' quarters.

This left David totally perplexed. What could he do? The news of Bathsheba's illegitimate child could not be allowed to get out, or his reputation, built up over the years with such sacrifice, would be ruined. As a last resort, he made a note to Joab instructing him to place Uriah in the heat of the battle, so that he would be killed.

Ironically, he handed the note to Uriah and asked him to deliver it to his general. Uriah faithfully complied with this request, Joab did as he was told, and the news soon came back that Uriah had died fighting in battle. David was now free to make Bathsheba his wife, and the child in her womb would gain legitimacy.

Bathsheba completed her time of pregnancy without further complication, and then she delivered their son. All seemed to be well for the moment, but God was not pleased with what David had done.

SIN CONFRONTED

Soon, the Lord sent the prophet Nathan to David, to confront him about this sin. Nathan told the king a story of a rich man who'd had plenty of flocks and herds, and yet he took the only lamb owned by a poor man and kept it for himself. David became furious when he heard the story. Who would do such a detestable thing? "Tell me who that man is," he offered. "I'll have him put to death, and the poor man's goods will be restored to him four times over."

There was a pause, and then the prophet responded, "You are the man, my king." As he said this, he was looking directly into the eyes of his monarch, and it created an eery silence.

Perhaps until that moment, David had continued to justify his actions, but now he suddenly saw them for just what they were. He had stolen a man's wife, and he had been a good man and a good friend. Then, to complicate that first sin, he had ordered that the man be killed to cover up what he had done first. How utterly detestable!

God had given him the kingdom, and he could have asked for whatever he wanted, and yet he had done this. How disgusting! At the time, his sin had seemed reasonable and even justifiable. Now the very thought of it sickened him.

It sickened God too, and Nathan had a message from Him for David. David would reap what he had sowed. He would experience continual war with his neighbors, there would be much trouble in his own household, and some of his wives would eventually be given to others. Because

At the time, David's sin had seemed reasonable and even justifiable. Now the very thought of it sickened him!

of what he had done secretly, everyone would know what happened to him.

There was more. Because of their sin, the child born to David and Bathsheba would die.

The accumulated impact of seeing his sin as it really was and knowing its full consequences brought David to his knees. He confessed to Nathan that he had sinned. He was grateful to God that his punishment was not even worse. God could have placed a death sentence upon David, but He had shown him mercy. Unfortunately, in the days to come, David would reap much heartache from this entire sad episode.

David Repented

In that moment, David could have gotten angry at God (as many do when rebuked and confronted with their wrongdoing) and become rebellious. Wasn't that exactly what Saul had done? And that king had never recovered from it. Rebelliousness had led him to other sins, and his sins had eventually separated him from God.

David chose a much wiser path. He admitted that he was wrong, an act we call repentance. As David was repenting, he sought the Lord and worshiped Him. To David, the most precious thing he possessed in life was the presence of the Lord, and he did not want to lose that. It was the presence of the Lord that had sustained him for so many years. Let God take from Him what He would. God was just and right. "But Lord," he prayed fervently, "please don't take Your Holy Spirit from me."

David never did become perfect, but he had a heart after God, and he was determined to serve Him, come what may. As a result, the call of God was wonderfully fulfilled in his life.

CHAPTER 3

COMPARING THE TWO KINGS

*Cast me not away from thy presence; and take not thy
holy spirit from me.*   Psalm 51:11

It's interesting to compare these two kings. Both Saul
and David were called of God, and they had the very same
high calling: to become king. For one reason or another,
they were both unlikely candidates and probably would
not have been chosen by men. They were both anointed
by the same man of God, the prophet Samuel, and were
the only kings he anointed in his lifetime. Both men started
out right, stepping into their call with great humility. Then,
as humans, they both had their failures.

THAT'S WHERE THE SIMILARITIES END

But that's where the similarities between these two
kings end. When confronted with their sin, their responses

could not have been more different. Saul blamed others, even refusing to admit that he had done anything wrong at all. David, on the other hand, abhorred his sin, took responsibility for it, and repented of it.

David was not perfect by any means, but he knew enough to run back to the Lord whenever he had "messed up"!

When Samuel confronted Saul at the altar, when he had become impatient and had not been willing to wait as instructed, the king only offered excuses for his sin. He also lied about his wrongdoing, blaming others, in defense of himself, when he had failed to complete the task that was given to him. Through his disobedience, Saul showed a lack of respect for Samuel and took upon himself authority that was not his. Then, he failed to have a repentant heart, and this led him further away from his goal. Rejecting God and His servant, Saul began to operate in his own strength.

When God rejected Saul and chose David to replace him, instead of changing his heart, Saul became obsessed with trying to kill David. All he cared about at that point was not losing his position as king.

When the prophet Nathan confronted David with his sin against Bathsheba and her husband, David quickly acknowledged that he had been wrong, repented, and turned his heart back to the Lord. He was not perfect by any means, but he knew enough to run back to the Lord whenever he had "messed up."

Psalm 51 Shows David's Heart

Psalm 51 shows us David's heart at the moment of his confrontation with Nathan. In the King James Version of the Bible, this psalm is labeled: "To the chief Musician, A Psalm of David, when Nathan the prophet came unto him, after he had gone in to Bathsheba." By reading the psalm, we catch a very intimate glimpse into exactly what David was feeling right then:

Have mercy upon me, O God, according to thy lovingkindness: according unto the multitude of thy tender mercies blot out my transgressions.
Wash me thoroughly from mine iniquity, and cleanse me from my sin.
For I acknowledge my transgressions: and my sin is ever before me.
Against thee, thee only, have I sinned, and done this evil in thy sight: that thou mightest be justified when thou speakest, and be clear when thou judgest.
Behold, I was shapen in iniquity; and in sin did my mother conceive me.
Behold, thou desirest truth in the inward parts: and in

the hidden part thou shalt make me to know wisdom.
Purge me with hyssop, and I shall be clean: wash me,
and I shall be whiter than snow.
Make me to hear joy and gladness; that the bones which
thou hast broken may rejoice.
Hide thy face from my sins, and blot out all mine iniq-
uities.
Create in me a clean heart, O God; and renew a right
spirit within me.
Cast me not away from thy presence; and take not thy
holy spirit from me.
Restore unto me the joy of thy salvation; and uphold
me with thy free spirit.
Then will I teach transgressors thy ways; and sinners
shall be converted unto thee.
Deliver me from bloodguiltiness, O God, thou God of
my salvation: and my tongue shall sing aloud of thy
righteousness.
O Lord, open thou my lips; and my mouth shall show
forth thy praise.
For thou desirest not sacrifice; else would I give it: thou
delightest not in burnt offering.
The sacrifices of God are a broken spirit: a broken and
a contrite heart, O God, thou wilt not despise.

Psalm 51:1-17

David had long been a man of praise and worship, and he refused to allow his own failure to interfere with his relationship with God. That's why, throughout his life-

COMPARING THE TWO KINGS

time, he was able to operate with strength from the Almighty.

David Was Not Threatened by Others

Unlike Saul, David was not threatened by others. When his son, Absalom, tried to take over the kingdom, David and his people were forced to flee from Jerusalem for safety. Their hope was that in time they could come back, but at the moment, it wasn't clear whether that would be possible or not.

It had long been David's custom to take the Ark of the Covenant along with him when he went out to any battle, and the priests now prepared it for travel. Seeing them with it in the roadway, David told them to take it back. If it was God's plan for him to continue as king, He would bring him back.[1]

Also unlike Saul, David was willing to give up his position, if God somehow required it. Being king was not the most important thing to him. Obeying God from day to day was much more important.

Why Is It Important?

Why is it even important to study these two kings? Because their lives affected many generations that followed them—for bad or for good. Saul brought a curse upon his family, and most of his sons died with him in battle.

David, to the contrary, received favor from God and a promise that his son Solomon would rule as the third king of Israel, would build a temple for the Lord in the Holy City, and that God's mercy would not leave Solomon as it had Saul.[2] David believed this promise, and so he thanked and worshiped God for it.[3]

The Scriptures show that Solomon loved the Lord, as his father David had before him.[4] And, just as God had promised David, He continued His plan through Solomon, David's son.

Saul was the first king of Israel and David the second, but after the death of both men, it was David who was honored. Despite his shortcomings, he was remembered as a man who worshiped and taught others to worship and as a man after God's own heart. Saul made his choices in life, and in the process, he lost all honor.

May these comparisons guide our own choices in life, for in doing so, we, also, choose blessing or cursing.

PART II

TWO SERVANTS

CHAPTER 4

ELISHA

But Jehoshaphat said, Is there not here a prophet of the LORD, that we may inquire of the LORD by him? And one of the king of Israel's servants answered and said, Here is Elisha the son of Shaphat, which poured water on the hands of Elijah.

2 Kings 3:11

When Elisha, the son of Shaphat, came on the scene, there was already a main character, God's prophet of the hour, at work. His name, of course, was Elijah. He was said to be a Tishbite, and he was doing great exploits among the people. For instance, with great courage, he challenged the prophets of Baal and called fire down from Heaven to prove who the real God was. Then he killed a large group of those false prophets.

ELIJAH BECAME DISCOURAGED

Interestingly enough, after this, which may well have been his greatest exploit, Elijah became frightened and discouraged and actually ran away in fear and hid. The ungodly Queen Jezebel, patron of the false prophets whom he had destroyed, had issued a death threat against him. Elijah, she said, would be dead within twenty-four hours.

While in hiding from Jezebel, Elijah became very discouraged. It appears that he even decided to give up being a prophet, not wishing to be in such a high profile position any longer.

ELIJAH'S PREVIOUS SERVANT

Elijah had a faithful man who traveled everywhere with him and served him, but while he was in this period of hiding from Jezebel, for some reason, the servant was left behind. It is not clear if Elijah abandoned his servant so that he could better hide himself, or if he ordered the servant to go away so as not to put *his* life at risk as well.

Other possibilities are that this was a test of the servant's faithfulness or that Elijah simply felt that the job had come to an end. Whatever the case, it appears that the two men never worked together again. But Elijah needed help, and God had the perfect man in mind for the job.

BEING SET UP FOR MINISTRY[1]

APPOINTED AND ANOINTED

For a time, it seemed that the prophet Elijah could not

get past his discouragement. Still, during this very time, God told him to go and anoint two kings and a prophet for their new positions. Because God had spoken it, Elijah didn't have to discuss the matter with anyone or get anyone's approval. God had spoken it, and it was up to Elijah to perform it.

The prophet whom Elijah was to anoint was a young man named Elisha, and he was the son of Shaphat of Abelmeholah. He was actually being chosen by God to take Elijah's place. God set up an appointment, a time when the two would meet (as if by accident), and Elijah would physically anoint the younger man for his position.

> *God had spoken it, and it was up to Elijah to perform it!*

Elisha, of course, would not become the prophet to the nation immediately. This particular anointing would begin his period of training at Elijah's side. If he proved faithful, he would, at some point, become the next official prophet to the nation.

THE CALL

As he had been instructed, Elijah went and found Elisha. This was no easy task. The younger man was found plowing in the field behind his twelve yoke of oxen. As Elijah walked past him, he threw his mantle, or wrap, over the shoulders of the plowman.

Elisha was apparently no novice. He knew who this man was, and he knew that this mantle, now being laid upon him, had been used to do many miracles. It represented the power of God, and that power was now being laid upon him.

Elisha immediately recognized the call of God upon his life. There were no trumpets to herald it, and no one was there to witness it (except Elijah), but it was real nevertheless. It was also life-changing.

THE ACCEPTANCE OF THE CALL

How did Elisha show his acceptance of God's call? He left his oxen (which represented considerable wealth) and ran after Elijah (who apparently had thrown the mantle upon the lad and then continued passing on). Elisha told Elijah that he would follow him. He requested only that he be allowed to properly say good-bye to his parents.

Elisha then did something rather startling. He killed one of his yoke of oxen, and, building a fire, cooked them (with the instruments still attached) and gave a feast to his friends and family. He may have tried, perhaps in vain, to explain to them what he was doing. Something had happened to him, and he felt an urgency to immediately change his profession. He would go after and serve the prophet Elijah.

In this way, by leaving behind his family and friends

and choosing to follow the prophet, Elisha showed his acceptance of the call. The killing of the oxen showed that he did not expect to change his mind and return to the past. Accepting the call had changed everything. God was speaking to him, and he could no longer remain the same.

A Serious Step of Faith

This must have horrified some or all of Elisha's friends and family members. After all, what he was doing was considered to be very risky. He seemed to have great-sounding plans, but how would it all come about? Clearly, Elisha was taking a serious step of faith. He was trusting God. If God sent the prophet this way and caused him to perform this important and meaningful act, then God must know what He was doing. From that moment, Elisha would look forward, never backward.

In some unspecified way, God had obviously prepared Elisha for this moment. There was something in his heart that had caused Elijah to pass his way in the first place. Apparently, God had already spoken to him, and he may well have already been going through a period of restless waiting, such as comes before the fulfillment of a call. It is this restlessness that many times turns into frustration and makes us ready to embrace change.

We should note that although God does not always require us to leave family or profession to accept His call, it will always change us dramatically.

As always, the call is very personal, and this is the reason many who are close to us are unable to understand it.

IN TRAINING AS A SERVANT

Elisha's first assignment (as part of his training for the call to be a prophet) was to become Elijah's servant. In this role, Elisha probably cooked for the older man, cleaned his shoes when they needed cleaning, and ran errands when there were errands to run. In short, he did whatever Elijah needed him to do. This must have seemed like a serious step down for a man who had owned so many yokes of oxen.

> *Serving in this humble way also must not have seemed like the thing a serious prophet to the nations should be doing!*

Serving in this humble way also must not have seemed like the thing a serious prophet to the nations should be doing, and that was exactly what Elisha's call had indicated. But becoming a faithful servant to another, especially to a mentor like Elijah, was just the first step in fulfilling his call. He could learn much at the master's side.

BECOMING THE PROPHET[2]

THE RESTLESS WAITING

God had spoken to Elijah that he would soon be taken up into Heaven by a whirlwind, and Elisha knew this. Then one day, as the two men were coming from Gilgal, the place of worship and sacrifice, Elijah said to his servant that the Lord was sending him on a journey. He would be saying his good-byes and making sure that all was in order. In the coming days, he would travel to Bethel, to Jericho, and to Jordan to speak with men whom everyone was calling *"the sons of the prophets"* (21 Kings 2:3). These were probably groups of students in training for the prophetic ministry, and Elijah was apparently their overseer.

Before traveling to each of these places, Elijah told Elisha to stay behind. Each time, however, Elisha's response was that he would not leave the older man. Until that moment, he had demonstrated humility and total submission to his mentor, but suddenly he seemed to be rebelling. Why would Elisha refuse to obey the prophet?

For one thing, Elisha understood that his first duty at the moment was to care for the prophet, and he didn't want to fail at that commission. So he had to accompany the prophet. Also, Elisha sensed that something important was about to take place, and he didn't want to miss it.

There may have been a third reason. If this final tour was putting closure on Elijah's life, it was important that Elisha understand the responsibilities he would be taking over. There were key people to be met in each of these places, and being with Elijah would enable Elisha to meet them. Therefore, he declined to stay at home.

When the prophet gave Elisha permission to stay behind, it was a test. This was his opportunity to get on with his life, if he so desired. But Elisha had no such desire. Fulfilling God's call *was* his life. He would not leave the prophet.

THE REACTION OF THE PROPHETIC STUDENTS

In the first two cities they visited, some of the students asked Elisha if he knew that the prophet would soon be leaving them. He told them he knew, as they did. They couldn't seem to understand why he was there. To them, Elisha was a servant about to be out of a job. They had probably heard about Elijah's previous servant, who was left behind and had to face an uncertain future. Why couldn't Elisha understand this? they apparently wondered.

Elisha guarded his heart and did not tell the students what God had spoken to him personally. They were in training for ministry themselves and might have been jealous, had Elisha revealed his call. He let them voice their opinions. He would focus on the instructions he had received from God, despite the fact that it made little sense to anyone else.

At every turn, Elisha was being tested. For his part, he was determined to do whatever it took to receive the fulfillment of the promise of his calling.

THE GREATER EXPECTATION

When they arrived at the Jordan River, fifty of those sons of the prophets stood back and watched the two men from a distance, and what they saw was startling.

Elijah took his mantle and struck the waters, and they divided so that he and Elisha could walk across the river on dry ground.

As they continued the journey, Elijah asked Elisha what he wanted from God before his master was taken from him. Elisha's response was that he wanted to receive double the anointing that Elijah had. This was asking a lot, and probably no one had been bold enough to ask it before. Elisha wanted to receive the things of God on a level he had not yet seen or heard of.

Elijah told the younger man very frankly that he had asked for a hard thing, and it would not easily be obtained. If Elisha could remain faithful and see him in the moment he was taken up into Heaven, God would grant that very bold desire of his heart. He would receive the anointing he desired, but it would come at an appointed time, and only if he obeyed the instructions he was given and then followed his call.

The Fulfillment of the Call

As they continued walking together, a chariot of fire and horses of fire suddenly appeared and moved between them, separating the two men. Elisha cried out, describing what he was seeing. Then a whirlwind took Elijah up into Heaven, and Elisha saw him no more.

It is notable that Elisha did not run in fear when the chariot and horses of fire appeared, even though he had never experienced anything like it before. He had been living for some time now in a state of expectancy, and so he fully expected to receive the promise, regardless of what it looked like or how it came. He was serious about the things of God and was open to receive whatever God would do.

NEEDED: REVELATION

When Elijah had said to the younger man, "If you see me when I'm taken, you will receive what you've asked for," he was probably not talking only of the natural sight of his leaving. If it had been only the natural sight that must be viewed, then it would have been simply a matter of Elisha keeping his eyes on the prophet constantly, never letting him out of his sight. Even that would have been difficult because a whirlwind could come very quickly and leave little time for turning the head. Elisha, therefore, must have kept his eyes glued on the prophet at all times, unable to rest even for a moment.

But surely Elijah had been speaking more of spiritual sight, revelation in the Spirit. Elisha must make the heavenly connection and see into the things of eternity. He was not only willing to do this; he knew he could do it. His deep hunger for the things of God had long been the controlling factor in his life.

Elisha's greatest desire was to follow God according to his calling, and in order to walk in the fullness of that calling, his spiritual eyes must be opened, and he must be able to hear from God and receive revelation. He was confident that he could to that.

As Elijah went up, his mantle fell from him and drifted toward the ground. Elisha quickly ripped his own coat open, tore it off, and threw it down, and then he picked up the fallen mantle of Elijah. The old had to be removed before the new could be embraced. The new would not fit over the old. Elisha had to let go of the past before he could embrace the future.

Elisha had first demonstrated his willingness to do this when he had killed his oxen and left his plow to follow his call. This had happened because the very same mantle had fallen over him. Leaving his old cloak lying there on the ground ripped in half, he adopting the mantle of Elijah as his new clothing.

The first time the mantle had been placed on him, it was done as a sign of his calling. He was called, but the mantle was not his to keep. It was a goal for him to work toward, the promise of what was to come. He had been anointed with it, but then he'd had to return it. It belonged to someone else, and he had no authority to put it to the test.

This time, the mantle was his. It was not taken as a souvenir, but as the promise of God that He would be with the prophet and do for him what He had done for

> *The old had to be removed before the new could be embraced!*

THE RESTLESSNESS OF THE CALL

his predecessor. God had been faithful to Elijah, and now He was fulfilling His promise to Elisha in the same way.

Stepping into the Call

When Elisha picked up that mantle, he had a decision to make. He had been given the promise that if he saw Elijah go up into Heaven what he desired would become his. Would he accept this mantle as the fulfillment of that promise? Or would he doubt and ask for some other sign? His mentor was now gone, and no one else was there to encourage him to take up the promise. Still, with confidence in what had already been spoken to him, Elisha took the mantle as his own and as the sign that God would indeed fulfill His word.

Action Required

Elisha, of course, did much more then just pick up the mantle. He quickly took hold of it, even though he had no guarantee that it would work for him as it had for Elijah, and he proceeded to do with it exactly what he had seen Elijah do before him. He went back to the spot where they had stood together by the Jordan River days before, and there he struck the water, declaring as he did so:

Where is the Lord God of Elijah?   2 Kings 2:14

Elisha was not a man to have a promise just for the sake of having it. If God had promised, then he wanted to see what God had promised. By striking the water as Elijah had, he was challenging that promise. He would not be afraid to use his anointing. He would take his promise and run with it.

Did it work? Immediately, the waters of the Jordan River parted, and Elisha walked across to the other side on dry ground.

It took courage for Elisha to use his promise for the first time. Until that moment, he had only been known as a servant. He had not proven his calling, to himself or to anyone else. This was his moment, and when he did what he needed to do, it worked.

This was a powerful first step into his calling, for the sons of the prophets were still watching him from a distance. When they saw him strike the water with the mantle and then they saw the water miraculously parting, they didn't hesitate to say to each other that the spirit that had been upon Elijah had now been transferred to Elisha.

Elisha didn't have to tell anyone about his anointing. It was quickly recognized. Even those who had ridiculed him or, at the very least, had not been willing to put their stamp of approval upon him now suddenly realized that things had changed. They may not have seen the chariot and horses of fire, but they saw the evidence of the passing of the anointing. When God was ready to fulfill His promise to Elisha, and Elisha was ready to receive it in faith, no one could stop it.

A VERY IMPORTANT POINT

This is a very important point. Elisha could not just sit around waiting for things to happen. There is a timing involved, and we cannot rush God. At the same time, we cannot just sit around and do nothing and expect to find our ultimate destiny. Something is required of us.

> *Elisha could not just sit around waiting for things to happen!*

When Elisha picked up the mantle from the ground, he could not just carry it around with him, hoping and praying that God would use him. He had to use it.

He knew it was the right season, so now it was up to him. It was the right time, and the death of Elijah was the triggering event for his rise to power and authority. Now that he had that authority in his hand, he had to do something with it. The action of Elisha brought on the fulfillment of his calling.

THE CALL ESTABLISHED

The sons of the prophets, who had been observing from a distance, now came and bowed before Elisha. In this way, they acknowledged his new authority and also when they asked if they could go and look for Elijah—just in case God had not delivered him to Heaven as promised. Elisha, who had personally witnessed Elijah's translation, had no doubt that God had completed the task. It wasn't necessary to go look for Elijah, he told them. He knew exactly where he was now.

The other men kept insisting ... until Elisha relented and let them go anyway. They had acknowledged his new authority in one sense, but in another, very real sense, they did not want to accept his answer. Instead, they insisted on having their own way.

So fifty men searched for three days for Elijah, and when they finally came back, they had not found him. It seemed that he was nowhere to be found (on earth, that is).

Elisha had waited for the men in Jericho, and when they returned, he told them that if they would have listened to him in the first place, they wouldn't have wasted so much time. He was quickly establishing his authority and learning how to be firm.

In the coming years, Elisha walked in authority among the people, doing many miracles. The people called upon him when they needed to hear from God, and in this way, they acknowledged him as the official prophet of the day. His calling had been established when he began faithfully walking in it.

ELISHA AS PROPHET

JUST THE BEGINNING

The revelation that Elisha received when Elijah was taken up to Heaven by horses and a chariot of fire was just the beginning of what God would show him in the days ahead. Once he had begun to receive revelation, he expected it to continue, and he expected to impart it to others.

The chariots and horses of fire were noted again later in Elisha's ministry, when, one day, he asked God to give his own servant spiritual vision.[3] The servant had gone out that morning, only to find that the hill where they lived in Dothan was surrounded by hostile forces. There were chariots and horses and a great host, so that the servant became alarmed and ran to tell Elisha.

Elisha was surprisingly calm about this news. He told his servant not to worry. Those who were *with* them were more than those who were *against* them. This may or may not have made sense to the servant, so Elisha then asked God to open the servant's eyes so that he could see into the spiritual realm and know what God Himself was doing about the situation.

Suddenly, because of Elisha's intercession, the servant was able to see the mountain full of horses and chariots of fire surrounding them. When he saw what was going on in the spirit realm, all fear left him. He understood, from that day forward, that this man Elisha walked in great favor with God.

ADVISING KINGS

Elisha not only began his ministry well; he continued to seek God and to be dependant upon the Lord. The second book of Kings records a story of three kings who needed divine guidance to wage a battle against a superior enemy. When they asked Elisha to help them, he called for a musician. The musician played and worshiped God, and as he did this, Elisha heard from God and began to prophesy, giving inspired instructions to the kings.[4] The kings received this word from God and obeyed it, and, consequently, they won the battle, without even fighting—just as Elisha had prophesied they would.

Elisha's job was not an easy one. At times, he was not well received, and the message he brought from God was not well received. Nevertheless, he carried a burden for Israel, even weeping when he sensed that evil was coming upon the nation.[5]

I have no doubt that Elisha sometimes knew what it was to be lonely. He traveled a lot, for that was his life, and he was often misunderstood. Loneliness, therefore, was just part of his call.

GOD'S PLAN FULFILLED

Elisha's reward came when he was able to remain faithful to his call until the end. Like everyone else, there was a process and timing involved in his call, and he had to walk it out. There were probably times when he wondered if perhaps he had "messed up" or missed God. He probably got homesick at times, or even discouraged, when it seemed that it was taking too long for things to happen. When things got tough, he had nothing to fall back on. That which made him great also made him vulnerable.

He had proved himself faithful by giving up all that he had and attaching himself to the prophet. In the process, he showed that he placed greater value on the things of God than he did on possessions. He had a heart for the Lord and believed that he would eventually receive his promise if he was obedient.

Elisha lived in humility following his call and refused to change for circumstance. His faith was tried, yet he remained faithful, focusing on what the Lord had said to him, even when it seemed to make no sense to others. When it seemed that he would soon be nothing more than a servant without a job, some gave him advice and others ridiculed him. They could not understand his calling or what God had spoken to him personally.

Elisha endured it all, sensing that God had much to teach him before moving him to another level. He trusted God and was determined to be faithful and hold steady until God brought it all to pass.

As a consequence, Elisha taught other prophets, advised kings, and did great miracles. Until his death, he remained a man of great influence.

Elisha's rather strange request for a double portion of the anointing that had resided upon Elijah was fulfilled, and the Scriptures record the fact that twice as many miracles were done in his life as had been done in the life of his predecessor.

In everything, Elisha remained faithful to God, and therefore, God's plan for his life was fulfilled.

CHAPTER 5

GEHAZI

Gehazi followed after Naaman.   2 Kings 5:21

After Elisha became the prophet, this man Gehazi became his servant. He lived with Elisha, went on journeys with him, and served him in every possible way—just as Elisha had done with Elijah. Gehazi must have been a good man, because he would not have been chosen for such an honored and trusted position if his attitude had not been good or if he had been unwilling to do God's will. This service to the prophet was a call, and it was a necessary preparation for greater things, as we saw in the last chapter with Elisha himself.

Gehazi was blessed in that he had before him a powerful example of faithfulness and determination in the person of Elisha. He knew about Elisha's faithful service to Elijah and his subsequent promotion. He, too, had a high calling, but first he must serve, desiring to ultimately fulfill the purpose that God had ordained for his life.

GEHAZI WAS USED TO BLESS THE SHUNAMITE WOMAN

THE WOMAN RECEIVED HER CHILD[1]

This shows us that Gehazi was also a man of compassion!

In their many travels, the prophet Elisha and his servant Gehazi passed through Shunem on a regular basis. A wealthy woman of that place invited them to eat with her and her husband whenever they passed through the city. She also prepared a room for them to stay in when they were in town. She believed that Elisha was a man of God, and she wanted to bless him.

The prophet wanted to return a blessing to her for all of her goodness, so he asked Gehazi to go get the woman. When she came, he asked her what they could do for her. Elisha suggested, for instance, that he could speak to the king or to the captain of the army on her behalf. She said that would not be necessary. Like most people who are led to bless God's servants, she didn't require anything in return.

Still, Elisha wanted to bless the woman, so he asked

Gehazi if he had any suggestions of how they might bless her. Gehazi noted that the couple had no children and that her husband was getting older. If they didn't have children soon, they wouldn't be able to have any. Surely they had a desire to have children of their own. This shows us that Gehazi was also a man of compassion. He, too, wanted this woman to be blessed, and he was able to come up with a way of blessing her.

The prophet liked the idea and sent Gehazi to get the woman again. When she came this time, Elisha told her that she was about to become pregnant, and she would have a son. As it turned out, this had been a deep desire of her heart. She was pleasantly shocked by this news and asked if it could be true. It was, Elisha assured her. God would do this thing for her.

And God did it. The woman became pregnant and eventually bore a son.

It's interesting to notice that the prophet had thought of natural favors, within his power to deliver, to bless the woman, while Gehazi considered something impossible in the natural. This servant would not have suggested a miracle if he had not believed in the power of God and that what he was suggesting could actually happen through the prophet. This shows his great respect for God and for the prophet of God. Gehazi was a good man with a good heart.

THE DEATH OF THE MIRACLE CHILD

After some time had passed, this miracle child, born to the Shunamite woman and her aging husband, became ill and died. Not despairing, she took his lifeless body and placed it on Elisha's bed and then shut the door. Then she asked her husband to send a servant with donkeys as quickly as possible to bring her to the prophet. Everything would be all right, she assured him.

She told the servant to go just as fast as the animals possibly could and not to stop for any reason, unless she told him to. He did that.

When they got close to Carmel, where the prophet was, he saw them coming from a distance and noticed how fast they were moving. He sent Gehazi to run and meet them. Obviously, something was wrong.

To Gehazi's inquiries, the woman only responded that all was well with her, her husband, and her child. Then she ran and wrapped her arms around the prophet's feet.

Gehazi, concerned for his master, tried to pull her away. Elisha told him to leave the woman alone. It was obvious that she was desperate.

When the woman finally confided in the prophet the fact that her son had died, Elisha told Gehazi to take his (Elisha's) staff and hurry to the child. He was to place the staff on the child's face. The woman, however, refused to go back without Elisha, and he prepared to accompany her.

In obedience, Gehazi ran ahead, and before the other two got there, he was returning to meet them. It didn't work, he said. The child was still dead.

When Elisha arrived at the house, he went into the room alone and prayed. After some time, the child was revived, and Elisha told Gehazi to bring the woman to get her child. She was thankful and took her son back to their quarters.

Gehazi's Part

Gehazi had been very much a part of her receiving her son years earlier, and now he had been involved in this situation too, but there were some warning signals along the way. Wanting to protect his master, Gehazi had tried to remove the woman and was told to leave her alone. When Elisha proposed sending Gehazi with the staff, the woman didn't acknowledge Gehazi as being part of the answer and refused to accept anything less than the presence of the prophet in her house where her dead child waited.

Gehazi obeyed the prophet, taking the staff that represented the power of God and laying it on the face of the child, but there was no result. Even with the staff of power in his hand, he had proved powerless in this situation. Either he didn't know how to use the anointing, God didn't honor his use of it, or the woman refused to receive his use of it.

This experience could have made Gehazi bitter. He had done all that was asked of him, and yet there was no result. When Elisha prayed, the child came back to life. This may have been hurtful to Gehazi and caused him to feel that he was of little value. God, who sees the hearts of all men, must have had other thoughts. We think we know what's in men's hearts, but He really knows.

THE WOMAN'S PROPERTY WAS RESTORED[2]

Later on, Elisha told the woman to move to another area to avoid the effects of a famine that was devastating her land. He sensed that it would be a long famine and that she would be better off elsewhere. The woman, with all of her household, did as the prophet had suggested, leaving the area and not coming back for seven years.

When the family returned to the area, the woman went to the king to request that her house and land be returned to her. When she arrived, Gehazi was there talking to the king. The king had asked Gehazi to tell him about some of the great miracles the prophet had done. As he was telling the king about the raising of the Shunamite's son to life again, he saw her arrive and pointed her out to the king. The king then asked the woman herself to tell him more about what God had done for her.

After talking to this woman for awhile, the king was so impressed that he restored not only all that was hers, but also all that her land had produced while she was away. In this way, the woman received more than she had dared hope for.

Once again, Gehazi was a part of causing the Shunamite woman to be blessed. He probably rejoiced about what had happened, for it was a day of victory and restoration for the woman and her household. But, Gehazi, who, when she arrived, had the attention of the king, had to step back while she was being heard and then blessed. He might have become jealous after she was asked to tell her own story, and he may well have felt left out when he did not receive any credit for the good done to the woman.

GEHAZI'S FAILURE[3]

NAAMAN WAS HEALED OF LEPROSY

Naaman, the captain of the army of Syria, was considered a very honorable and mighty man, but he suffered from leprosy. Then one day his Israelite maid told Naaman's wife that if he would go to the prophet in Israel he would be healed. The Syrian king sent Naaman with a letter addressed to the king of Israel, asking for healing for his captain.

When Naaman arrived with this letter, the king of Israel was upset and thought the man was just trying to start some kind of trouble. What did he know about healing people? Elisha heard about this and sent word to the king to let the man come to him. God, he said, would prove Himself to their pagan neighbors through this miracle.

When Naaman arrived at the house of Elisha, it was Gehazi who was sent out to greet him!

When Naaman arrived at the house of Elisha, it was Gehazi who was sent out to greet him. He bore a message for Naaman. If he would wash in the Jordan River seven times, he would be healed. Naaman, an important official, was offended by the lack of protocol. Elisha should have come out and done some sort of religious ceremony, he felt.

In time, Naaman's servants convinced him that he had nothing to lose by doing what the prophet had said. So he did. He went to the Jordan River, and there he dipped seven times. And, sure enough, he was healed.

Naaman was so thankful that he went back to Elisha's house to acknowledge God and His servant and to give him some appropriate (and valuable) gifts. Strangely enough, Elisha refused to receive any of the gifts, and Naaman left for home, no doubt a little offended and a little perplexed by it all.

GEHAZI'S HEART WAS REVEALED

Before Naaman had gotten very far away, Gehazi ran after him. Seeing the servant coming, Naaman stopped to see what he wanted. Gehazi said that Elisha had changed his mind and *would* receive a few of the gifts Naaman had offered. Two young men of the sons of the prophets were on their way to see them even then, and they would need some provisions. It was, of course, all an elaborate lie.

Naaman was only too happy to comply. He gave Gehazi twice as much money as he asked for and two sets of clothing. It was more than Gehazi could carry, so Naaman sent two of his servants to carry it. When they got close to the house, Gehazi took the loot and hid it, and then he went inside.

GEHAZI

When Gehazi came inside, Elisha asked him where he'd been. Gehazi lied again, to cover up his first wrong, saying that he had not gone anywhere at all. Elisha knew this was not the truth. His heart had gone with the servant, and he knew (and God knew) exactly what he had done.

This sin committed by Gehazi was so distasteful to God and to His prophet that Elisha now declared a curse upon his formerly faithful servant. The leprosy that had been upon Naaman would now be upon him. In that moment, Gehazi was suddenly leprous, and he withdrew from Elisha's presence. He was to die in that wretched state.

Why?

What would have caused Gehazi to do such a rash and abhorrent thing? Perhaps he was offended because Elisha had turned down the gifts, and there would have been something there that blessed him too. Of course, God had his reasons for telling Elisha to refuse the gifts, and Elisha would not have needlessly offended such a powerful man as Naaman.

Apparently Gehazi resented the decision and somehow felt that it was unfair to him. Misunderstandings over money are not an uncommon occurrence in ministry, but there is a way to handle such misunderstandings. And this was clearly not the way.

Probably, more to the point, Gehazi, for some reason, coveted these gifts. He plotted for his own gain, and then he justified his actions. He had been around Elisha long enough to know that he heard from God, so why did he think he could get away with such a falsehood? Sin somehow blinds the soul and makes us believe, not only that we're right, but also that we'll never be caught.

Gehazi's reasoning was not unusual. After all, Naaman wanted to give the gifts and had come a long way to show his appreciation. He was disappointed, and possibly even a little offended, when the gifts were refused. What would it hurt for Gehazi to take just a little of what had been offered?

Gehazi, for some reason, coveted these gifts!

Maybe Gehazi thought he was so close to Elisha and so needed by him that the man of God would never dare confront him or dismiss him. And the act of dismissal might well have been difficult for Elisha, but God seemed to have no problem with it. Quite possibly, this man Gehazi was in training as the next prophet of Israel, and he had just now failed the test, failed so miserably that he could not recover.

Gehazi had not only lied and deceived and stolen. He had gone against a decision made by the man who was over him in the Lord, and he had taken upon himself authority that was not his.

DID THE PUNISHMENT FIT THE CRIME?

Judging from the severity of his punishment, it seems very possible that Gehazi had allowed the restlessness of the call to overpower him. He had taken things into his own hands, taking for himself what Elisha had not been willing to give him. This was an outward sign of an inward rebellion, and God could not permit this in a person with such great potential.

Especially by modern standards, in a world devoid of discipline, the punishment meted out to Gehazi seems extreme. Did it fit the crime? Since it was God Himself who meted out the punishment, we have to believe that He knew more than we do. A man's heart does not change overnight, and this was probably not the first sign of a rebellious spirit in Gehazi. Apparently, over the years, this servant had allowed some hurts and offenses to build up in his heart. Refusing to lay them on the altar and give them to the Lord, he had allowed them to fester and contaminate his heart. When the test came, the true content of his heart was revealed.

LOSING SIGHT OF THE CALL

GEHAZI WAS NOT A NOVICE

At this point, Gehazi was not a novice. He had been under the prophet now for some years and knew his teachings well. He had not only heard Elisha teach; he had also seen him performing miracles, even being able to share in those miracles—as we have seen. Through accompanying Elisha, he had met many important leaders and had become comfortable in the presence of authority. Gehazi was clearly much more than just a servant to Elisha.

It was Gehazi himself who stood before the king without fear, testifying of Elisha's miracles. He had learned to be obedient and quick to respond to Elisha's requests. He was intelligent and able to remember and communicate messages that Elisha sent him to deliver to other people. He seemed to understand the ministry. He had so much going for him.

GOD'S PLAN WENT UNFULFILLED

It was not, in any way, God's plan for Gehazi to die as a leper, and it was not God's fault that this was to become his end. After years of faithfully serving the prophet, Gehazi's heart had changed, and he was no longer the man he had been at the beginning.

Gehazi was called to be a servant, but, according to the pattern we have seen developing in the Scriptures, it seems very probable that God's plan was to promote him far beyond that position. Even as a servant, Gehazi could have had opportunity to move to other spiritual levels. None of this happened because the issues of his heart intruded on his destiny. Sadly, in the end, the plan of God for Gehazi's life went unfulfilled.

CHAPTER 6

COMPARING THE TWO SERVANTS

For whether is greater, he that sitteth at meat, or he that serveth? is not he that sitteth at meat? but I am among you as he that serveth.   Luke 22:27

As a servant, Elisha proved himself faithful over time. Even when it seemed that he was a servant about to lose his job, he remained faithful. People gave their opinion when they didn't understand his call, but he died to himself, so that he could remain focused on what God was saying to him and how He was leading him. As a result, he received what he had asked from the Lord, a double portion of His Spirit. From the beginning, Elisha had a great desire for the things of the Lord and was determined to win them at all costs.

GEHAZI LOST SIGHT OF THE CALL

In contrast, Gehazi lost sight of the call after he had begun to resent being a servant. He failed to keep his heart pure, but allowed unresolved issues to remain there, and this gave rise to bitterness. The true condition of his heart was revealed when he lied, plotted, and went against the authority of his leader, undermining his decision. The heart issue that led to his downfall did not happen overnight. At some point, he went from serving with a heart toward God to serving out of duty only, and it was all downhill from there.

Elisha and Gehazi both had a high calling, but they were also both called to be servants first. Elisha proved faithful to God in every test, and these ultimately brought him from being a servant to stepping into his call, actually becoming a prophet. His reward was a life of usefulness and respect among his peers.

Gehazi lost sight of his call when he failed to deal with his issues by giving them to God. Being faithful for a long time would have brought great reward to him too—if his heart had been in order. Tragically, his reward was death.

JESUS IS OUR EXAMPLE

As Christians, Jesus is our greatest example of servanthood and humility. He was the very Son of God, God in the flesh, a great teacher, miracle worker, and leader, and yet He insisted on washing the disciples' feet. In that day, the people normally wore sandals and walked on very dusty roads. The washing of the feet, therefore, was an important duty, but it was carried out by the lowliest of servants.

At the end of His last supper with the disciples, Jesus washed their feet. Then He told them they must take His example and be servants to those around them. He had given them power, but that power would have little effect if they did not humble themselves and compassionately serve.

To be like Jesus, we must take on His heart and become a servant. That's the only way for us to win our battles.

BEING A SERVANT ISN'T EASY

At times, being a servant can be very difficult. Most of the honor and attention is placed on the leader, and very little credit, or recognition, is given to those who work hard in the background, causing things to happen. When we go unnoticed and unappreciated (or we think we're unappreciated), it can lead to feelings of being left out and taken advantage of. Therefore, as servants, we must always remind ourselves of why

> *Regardless of how great your call, you must first take on a servant's heart and serve as unto the Lord!*

we're doing what we're doing and Whom we're doing it for.

Regardless of how great your call, you must first take on a servant's heart and serve as unto the Lord in order to ultimately and totally fulfill God's plan and purpose for your life.

It seems obvious that the end of Gehazi's life could have been as glorious as that of Elisha. It was not God's fault. It was due to his own wrong choices. See that you choose well.

PART III

TWO PROPHETS

CHAPTER 7

ABRAHAM

He [Abraham] staggered not at the promise of God through unbelief; but was strong in faith, giving glory to God.   Romans 4:20

We don't usually think of Abraham as a prophet, but he was. At the age of seventy-five, God called this man, then called Abram, to leave his home town, Ur, and to go in search of a new city.[1] In the process, God promised to bless him and to make of him a great nation. Regardless of how great your call, you must first take on a servant's heart and serve as unto the Lord.[2]

In obedience to God, Abram, along with his wife Sarai and a few other family members, left their land and began a journey toward the land of Canaan, which God promised to give his heirs. There, Abram built his first altar and worshiped the Lord.

Abram's lie, used to protect himself from losing his wife, turned on him and caused him to lose the very thing he was trying to protect!

FEAR BRINGS FAILURE[3]

After they had lived in Canaan for a time, a famine arose in the land, and Abram took his household to Egypt to find provisions. Sarai was so beautiful and desirable that he was afraid someone there would kill him to have her. He told her to lie and say that she was his sister. It was a part truth. She was his half-sister, but she was also his wife, and what they were doing was deceitful.

Believing the lie, that Sarai was Abram's sister, Pharaoh took her as his wife and paid Abram well for her. But then God plagued Pharaoh's house because he had taken another man's wife. Abram's lie, used to protect himself from losing his life, turned on him and caused him to lose his wife, the very thing he was trying to protect. Out of fear, he had made a wrong decision, and now he regretted it. But was it too late?

THE PLAN RESTORED[4]

At the moment, it looked like God's plan for Abraham and his descendants was really "messed up," and only His mercy intervened. Before it was too late, Pharaoh realized that Sarai was Abram's wife, and he called Abram to come and take her back. How could the man have deceived him so? Only God's mercy had kept him from making her his wife for good.

Reunited again, Abram and Sarai were officially deported, put out of Egypt. They went back to the place where Abram had first built the altar, and there he rededicated himself to God.[5]

A COVENANT MADE[6]

When he had reached the ripe old age of ninety, Abram had his name changed by God. It would no longer be Abram, but Abraham, meaning *"a father of many nations"* (Genesis 17:5). At the same time, God also changed Sarai's name to Sarah, meaning *"a mother of nations"* (Genesis 17:16). No more unlikely couple could have been chosen for this role.

At the same time He changed Abram's name, God renewed His promise to Abraham and made a covenant with him for all future generations. But none of this seemed to make any sense because Abram (now Abraham) and Sarai (now Sarah), although they had been married for many years, were unable to have children. If they hadn't been able to bear children to this point, how could they be expected to bear them now?

Still, when God said it, Abraham believed it, and he consistently clung to that promise. Now fifteen years had passed since they had left their homeland, and Abraham and Sarah were still following God's plan and doing His will on a daily basis.

FEAR BRINGS FAILURE AGAIN[7]

Now Abraham and Sarah traveled to Gerar, and, as before, Abraham began to worry about losing his life because of Sarah's beauty. He knew better, but again Abraham lied and told the king of Gerar, King Abimelech, that Sarah was his sister. As a result, the very same thing happened again.

King Abimelech, taken by Sarah's great beauty, sent for her, and took her to be his wife, and God's plan was once again off track because of Abraham's failure. The *father of nations,* and the *mother of nations* were again separated, without hope of restoration, because of Abraham's fears.

You would think that Abraham would have learned his lesson the first time, but he fell into the very same trap again—all because he was afraid for his life. He had trusted God for years for a child, and yet here he was struggling to trust God to protect him to fulfill the promise.

THE PLAN RESTORED AGAIN[8]

Once again, God was forced to intervene and come to Abraham's rescue. He did it by revealing to the king in a dream that Sarah was Abraham's wife, and He told the king that he would die if he touched her or kept her as his own. Immediately his existing wife and his maidservants were all struck with barrenness.

The next day, the king told his servants about the dream, and they were all afraid when they heard that God's judgment could come upon them because of this. The king called for Abraham and confronted him with his treachery. Abraham humbly confessed all, and the king, after rebuking him, gave Sarah back to him, along with many gifts.

One of the gifts the king gave Abraham that day was enough money to buy Sarah a veil to hide her beauty. If she was covered in this way, he said, it would show anyone concerned that she was already taken as Abraham's wife. From then on, Abraham would not have to fear to openly speak the truth about her. It was a simple solution, one that Abraham should have thought of himself.

But God had also told the king something else, something startling—that Abraham was a prophet. If he would ask Abraham to pray for him, he would live. The king obeyed, Abraham prayed for him, and God healed his wife and maidservants from the barrenness that had resulted from taking another man's wife into his home. God had supernaturally restored things to their intended situation, for the king and for Abraham.

Humility and Healing

As king, this man had power to take Abraham's life for what he had done, but God humbled him when he told him that Abraham was a prophet. Instead of kill-ing him, he should ask Abraham for prayer. To ask a man who had wronged him in this way to pray for him was almost certainly a new revelation to this king. But he obeyed.

Abraham was also humbled before God when he was called upon to pray for the man he had wronged. The fact that he humbled himself before the king and prayed for him tells us that his heart was turned to God, for God had already dealt with him. Abraham, although he had to be confronted for his failure, was still the person whom God had anointed and called to be a prophet. His failure did not remove the call from his life. God used him that same day in a miracle of healing.

Abraham had "messed up" and probably thought he had lost his wife forever. What a tragedy that would have been! But what seemed hopeless changed, and just that quickly, God's plan was back on track. At the age of one hundred, Abraham and Sarah finally re-ceived their promised child. They named him Isaac.[9]

FAILURE AND THE CALL

Even though Abraham had failed (and more than once), God didn't take away his call to be a mighty prophet or His promise of blessings on his family—present and future. Abraham spent time at the altar with a repentant heart, and he used his failures to determine that he would do what God had called him to do in the future. Then he went on to become a pillar of faith who would inspire all succeeding generations.

God called Abraham His friend.[10] In the New Testament, Paul wrote of him that he was *"strong in faith, giving glory to God"* (Romans 4:20). Thankfully, for all of us who call ourselves the children of Abraham by faith, Abraham's story had a happy ending.

CHAPTER 8

MOSES

And there arose not a prophet since in Israel like unto Moses, whom the Lord knew face to face.

Deuteronomy 34:10

After several generations of God's people had lived and prospered in the land, they began to intermarry with the heathen and were in danger of losing their distinctiveness. God raised up Joseph (son of Jacob, son of Isaac, son of Abraham) and sent him to Egypt, where he became a respected official under the Pharaoh.

This happened because the whole world was threatened by famine, and Joseph, having a heart toward God, had prepared himself in dreams and visions. His interpretation of the Pharaoh's dreams moved him into the role of prime minister overnight.

During that great famine, God also moved the entire nation of Israel to Egypt. Their plan was to find provisions for the remaining years of the famine, but God's plan was to preserve them as a holy nation. They were to remain in Egypt for the next four hundred years.

In time, a new king arose over Egypt, and he did not know Joseph. Because the Israelites, over time, became mighty, this new king felt threatened by them and decided to make them slaves to the Egyptians. He also tried to kill all the baby Hebrew boys to reduce any future threat.

It was during this extremely critical time that Moses was born, and he was miraculously spared from the carnage by being adopted by Pharaoh's daughter. At an early age, therefore, he went to live in the palace, and it was Pharaoh's daughter who named him Moses, meaning "drawn from the water" (see Exodus 2:10).

Moses Was Born for a Purpose

Moses was born and his life was spared for a purpose. That purpose was to deliver the Israelites out of Egypt. This was his call, and it was ever before him— although he lived as a royal.

When Moses was forty years old, he went out of the palace one day to visit his brethren. On his way, he saw an Egyptian taskmaster beating an Israelite slave. The deliverer spirit rose up in him, and the urge to deliver his people so overwhelmed him that he fought with the taskmaster, unintentionally killing him in the process. It was not yet God's time for Moses to step into his call to be the deliverer, but in his restlessness, he stepped out in his own strength, and the result was disastrous.

To save his life, Moses was forced to run away (into the wilderness), and he remained there for the next forty years. There he married the daughter of a Midianite priest, and there he was mentored by his father-in-law, a man named Jethro.

Moses was born and his life was spared for a purpose!

In time, that king of Egypt died, and the Israelites in bondage in Egypt began to cry out to God for a deliverer. Moses was now eighty years old, and God had been preparing him to be His prophet. Now God would use him to deliver the children of Israel out of Egyptian bondage.

While Moses was herding his father-in-law's flock one day, the angel of the Lord appeared to him in a burning bush that was, miraculously, not consumed. The angel told Moses that God was sending him to Pharaoh to bring forth His people out of Egypt. The land of Canaan, which God had promised to Abraham, could now become theirs. His previous failure had not taken away the call of God that was upon his life.

FORTY YEARS HAD PASSED

Forty years had passed, and it must have appeared to Moses, at times, that what God had placed in his heart would never happen. But when the timing was right, and God felt that Moses was ready, the burning bush was the triggering event, and everything changed within a very short period of time.

After a long discussion with God regarding how inadequate he felt and how difficult it would be for him to walk in such authority, Moses said yes to God. God told him that the rod he had carried for years as a shepherd would now become his sign of authority and power from on high, and it would become known as *"the rod of God"* (Exodus 4:20). Moses knew that his own strength was not enough. It hadn't worked before, and it could not work now. This time, he would step out in obedience to God, believing that He would cause him to be successful in this impossible mission He had sent him on.

This was the same Moses, whom the Israelites had rejected years before. What did he know about slavery, having grown up in the palace? Now, God was sending him back to be their deliverer and also their ruler, and they would follow him.

GOD SET UP A MEETING

God set up a meeting in the wilderness between Moses and Aaron, Moses' natural brother. Aaron took the message of deliverance and the signs to the elders of the children of Israel, and they all believed and accepted that

God had sent Moses. God had said He would raise up one of their brethren as a prophet to be their deliverer, and it was unlikely that one of the Israelite slaves would be allowed to stand before Pharaoh in their defense. But, because Moses had been adopted into the royal family, he had access to Pharaoh and to the palace. He was well learned and could easily stand before the king and communicate, and he also knew the proper protocol for what needed to be said and done.

What God had done years earlier by placing Moses in the palace was certainly part of the plan of setting him up for the deliverance of His people. Then, during those forty years in the desert, Moses had been groomed in leadership and taught how to survive in that difficult environment. He would need this experience when taking the Israelites into the wilderness. So God had known what He was doing from the time Moses was born. Even though he'd had his failures, he was still chosen by God for this high purpose.

MOSES' PURPOSE FULFILLED

Like all of us, Moses had been born with a purpose. His purpose was to become the deliverer of the children of Israel. In the process of learning his place, he had killed a man, and that was wrong, but that personal failure did not change or remove his calling or purpose. He would be the deliverer—if he was still willing. And, thank God, he was.

Yes, Moses had to pay for his sins, but he was still able to fulfill God's plan for his life because he had said *yes* to God. If Moses could be used by God, you and I can be used too. Say *yes* to Him today.

CHAPTER 9

THE ULTIMATE CAUSE OF RESTLESSNESS

For the gifts and calling of God are without repentance.   Romans 11:29

Most of our restlessness, when it concerns ministry, is caused by the need for us to wait on God's timing and the fact that we can't understand that timing. We often feel we're ready, and God knows that we're not. But the ultimate cause of restlessness is our own failure.

HUMANS FAIL

Humans fail, and there is a tendency among us, when failure presents itself, to forget just how able God is to restore men and women, how loving and kind He is, and how strong His will is to give us hope, not condemnation.

When God calls us, He never makes the mistake of thinking that we're somehow perfect. He's God, and He knows very well that those to whom He is entrusting His Kingdom are frail creatures. His hope is that we will look to Him for our strength, and that when we fail, we will turn to Him for help. He never turns a deaf ear to those who call to Him.

Many of the truly great leaders of the Bible failed at some point in their lives!

Failure in your life can bring on one of two reactions. You can be forgiven and receive an even greater determination to win over your weaknesses, or you can become hopeless and let yourself fall into the pit of self-doubt and self-recrimination. The choice is yours.

Many of the truly great leaders of the Bible failed at some point in their lives, but they went on to become great because they didn't stay down. They got up and ran back to God, seeking His forgiveness and His help not to repeat the failure again. Dealing with their failures put a fight in their spirit and caused them to become overcomers.

No failure must be allowed to determine the outcome of this battle. Die to self, become dependent upon God for your needs, and you, too, can become a hero of the faith and a pillar of the Church.

THE ULTIMATE CAUSE OF RESTLESSNESS

Every Man Must Become a Continuing Work in the Master's Hand

In a general sense, we're all undeserving of God's blessings and restoration. The Scriptures state:

But we are all as an unclean thing, and all our righteousnesses are as filthy rags.   Isaiah 64:6

Because of this, every man must be a continuing work in the Master's hand. We can never earn the favor of God through religious works or self-sacrifice. We must cast ourselves upon His mercy daily.

But even when failure comes, the call never goes away. If our hearts are somehow turned away from God, the anointing may be taken from us, as it was from King Saul.[1] Yet, if and when men and women lay their lives on the altar and truly repent, God will always hear their cry. As our loving heavenly Father, He always calls His children back to Himself. It is up to us to decide if and when we will come back.

When God calls back an erring child, it's because He wants to restore their anointing and get the plan for their lives back on track. Let Him do this for you.

Our Feelings of Guilt

Feelings of guilt can sometimes cause us to turn away from our calling. After all, if we're so sinful, how can God use us any longer? But who among us is not sinful? We

155

may, therefore, condemn ourselves, but God will never condemn us. His Word declares:

> *There is therefore now NO CONDEMNATION to them which are in Christ Jesus, who walk not after the flesh, but after the Spirit.*   Romans 8:1, Emphasis Added

There is nothing here to indicate that we have to be perfect. We just need to be *"in Christ Jesus."* The writer of the Hebrews concluded:

> *Let us therefore come boldly unto the throne of grace, that we may obtain mercy, and find grace to help in time of need.*   Hebrews 4:16

This is all that God requires of us. If our heart is pure, we can stand as God's child and expect Him to use us just as He did Abraham. Don't forget that he failed and then almost immediately turned around and ministered to a king.[2]

John wrote:

> *If our heart condemn us not, then have we confidence toward God.*   1 John 3:21

The power comes from God, and not through our own abilities or strength. So our failures don't change the situation.

FAILURE IS UNIVERSAL

As we saw in Part I of this book, King David, a mighty man of God, failed and committed adultery with Bathsheba. Besides their affair and their illegitimate child, David arranged for Bathsheba's husband to be placed in the heat of the battle where he would die. Surely, when he first glimpsed Bathsheba and the thought came to him to sin with her, he never imagined what all that thought would lead to. With sin, things just have a way of getting out of control, or snowballing, on us.

Then David convinced himself of the necessity to cover his sin, and he felt bad about the resulting situation, but there was something else important to deal with. Just sweeping his sin under the rug didn't resolve anything. A man was dead, his wife was stolen, and David was trying to feel good about it all. The important thing was that a stronghold was taking shape in his heart, and if he didn't do something about it, it would eventually separate him from God. That was exactly what had happened to Saul.

Now God sent the prophet Nathan to confront the sin in David's life and bring him to true repentance. With that, David could get back on track to fulfill God's plan. David not only asked God to forgive him; he wanted a complete attitude adjustment. He prayed:

Create in me a clean heart, O God; and renew a right spirit within me.   Psalm 51:10

Because of the law of sowing and reaping, David paid for his sin with the loss of their first son, a loss of peace in the kingdom, and trouble in his own household.[3] Bathsheba, who was married to another man, had not been part of the original plan, but had become David's wife through sin. But when David truly repented and their hearts turned back to God, Bathsheba was grafted into the plan, and God blessed their union.

After this, Bathsheba bore David a second child. His name was Solomon, and he became the next king of Israel and built the great Temple of Solomon in Jerusalem.[4]

David's failure did not take away the call of God upon his life. In spite of every failure, he had a deep love for God and a heart after Him that kept him moving forward spiritually.

INTENTIONAL AND UNINTENTIONAL FAILURE

All great men of God have to face past failures. Life has its disappointments, and it's human nature to make wrong decisions from time to time. Some are made willingly and some are made unintentionally. In the story of Abraham, King Abimelech was innocent in taking Sarah for a wife, but Abraham was not innocent in the matter, for he had caused the king to think she was only his sister. Abraham's sin was willful, while Abimelech's was unknowing.

David also sinned willfully. He knew what he was doing when he had the affair and when he tried to cover it up.

Moses, before he started his ministry, had some anger issues to deal with. This caused him to accidentally kill a man, and he had to live on the run for many years to come. Years later, unfortunately, after God had used him so mightily to deliver the children of Israel out of Egypt, Moses again had a problem with his anger. This time, it kept him from entering the Promised Land. His anger brought about disobedience.[5] He should have dealt with these issues when he had the opportunity.[6] His failure to do so robbed him of his final blessing and his continued opportunity.

David paid for his sin!

Moses was still a great man, one who loved God, but he sold himself short on what God would have done in his life. God, the Creator of the universe, is powerful enough to take care of any man's situation and meet him right where he is. God can still fulfill His plan in anyone who will go after Him with a repentant heart—regardless of how badly they have failed in the past.

MAKE THE NECESSARY ADJUSTMENTS

How you respond to failure will ultimately determine if you can make adjustments in your life and better yourself. Always remember that your purpose and call does not change with the failure. The God of restoration can fulfill His plan through you—despite any and all personal failures.

THE RESTLESSNESS OF THE CALL

We men and women have enough of the nature of God in us that we want to bless our own, even when they fail. Children can be disobedient and then quickly run to those close to them and expect love in return. As undeserving as they may be, at Christmas, on birthdays or other special days, they're showered with gifts and love. How much more does God want to bless and do the same for His beloved children? He is a loving God who forgives, restores, and gives hope.

Your past must never be allowed to determine your future with God, for He is the God of healing and miracles. When you allow Him to restore you, healing from past hurts take place, walls fall down, and anything again becomes possible. God will still give you the abundance of spiritual blessings He has promised. He said:

> But if from thence thou shalt seek the Lord thy God, thou shalt find him, if thou seek him with all thy heart and with all thy soul. Deuteronomy 4:29

God will fulfill His plan in any man, woman, boy, or girl who truly goes after Him. What greater message of hope could we ask for?

PART IV

WHAT NOW?

CHAPTER 10

NOW, IT'S UP TO YOU

And Moses answered and said, But, behold, they will not believe me, nor hearken unto my voice: for they will say, The LORD hath not appeared unto thee.

O my Lord, I am not eloquent, ... but I am slow of speech.

And the LORD said unto him, Who hath made man's mouth? ... Now therefore go, and I will be with thy mouth, and teach thee what thou shalt say.

Exodus 4:1 and 10-12

Much can be learned by studying the lives of the people of the Bible. Why? Because people were the same then as they are now. Their times and culture may have been different, but their heart was the same. And God is also the same as He was way back then.

THE DRIVING FORCE TO SUCCEED

Men of great influence did not start out that way—then or now. There is always within those who succeed a driving force that keeps them striving onward until they are, at last, able to fulfill their purpose. It doesn't come overnight, but they keep doing God's will, walking daily through the process of training, following His leading for that particular day, and doing what He says. This process, which is absolutely necessary to step into an established call, can be a very long one. Many years are often spent in training, and during those years, sometimes we have only occasional glimpses of what God is doing. Just when we think we're ready to do great exploits, it turns out that we're not yet ready at all, and we have to go back to our training again.

Usually there is too much of our own strength in the mix, and we start out depending upon our own abilities. Then, when it seems that our destiny will never happen, and we cannot do any more in our own strength, that's when God steps in.

When God says it's time, then it's time, and nothing and no one can stop us. Until that moment, it's just not time yet.

Over time, trust on our part brings dependence upon God for the outcome. But each step of the call is an important one, and each serves a definite purpose. All of the pieces eventually fit together to form the whole plan.

In the excitement of the call, we cannot help God by rushing the plan. Like a cocoon that is prematurely broken open, we sometimes fail by trying to exist in our own strength or with the help of others. We simply cannot stand the test before we're ready. The waiting can be discouraging, but going ahead of God can also bring great disaster.

UNDERSTANDING QUALIFICATIONS

God qualifies those whom He has chosen. This is contrary to our thinking. We think that the qualified will always be chosen, but it's the other way around.

> *God qualifies those whom He has chosen!*

Unlike some of his brothers, David had no experience or other qualifications that would make someone think of him as a candidate for the position of king. Because he was young (and because it was highly unlikely that he would be needed in a meeting with the prophet Samuel), his father didn't even see the need to include him. It was to everyone's surprise that, when he was finally called in, he was immediately anointed to be the next king. It happened by God's direction through the prophet. Men would surely have made a very different choice.

Get used to it. God's qualifications are very different from our own.

Understanding Feelings of Inadequacy

Great men and women have accountability and responsibility before God, and yet even those who are willing vessels and have a total dependence upon the Lord often feel inadequate in their calling. They are reluctant because they see themselves through their own eyes and not as God sees them. Saul hid when Samuel was announcing to the people that God had appointed him as the first king over Israel, and you may feel like hiding too.

God will do the work, as inadequate as we might feel, if we will just be obedient to Him and take courage to do exactly what He says. This requires trust and confidence in God that He will perform what He has said He would do.

Moses, after years of preparation, was still afraid that no one would listen to him or believe that God had sent him. He even felt inadequate in his ability to speak before others. God told him that he was not going in his own power but with the authority of the Almighty. In this way, He let Moses know that it was not about him; it was about God's plan. God would make up for his inadequacies, and He'll do the same for you.

Understanding the Relationship Between Expectation and Reality

When the call is finally established, it rarely looks like what we expected. When God speaks, it's normal for us to associate His words with something we have seen or known in the past. What He envisions may be something entirely different.

Elisha asked for something beyond what he had seen when he asked for twice as much anointing as Elijah had. Elijah, who was known to be a great man of God and who did many miracles, possibly had never realized that he could ask for more than he'd already received. Elisha's seemingly impossible and unheard of request brought hard places and trials to his life, but his vision and expectation ultimately led him to a place beyond that which others of his time thought possible.

UNDERSTANDING TRIGGERING EVENTS

The establishment of the call usually seems to come suddenly, and this happens through some triggering event God has set up. Saul's calling kicked in when there was a crisis in the nation. The enemy had come against his people, and there seemed to be no hope for them. At that point, he rose up and led the people.

For David, being King of Judah was a step in his calling, but the established call was fulfilled suddenly when Israel's ungodly King Ishbosheth died, and David was asked to become King of all Israel.

Moses lived in the wilderness for forty years, and then, when he had the burning bush experience at the age of eighty, everything changed for him almost overnight.

Elisha went from being a servant about to be out of a job to picking up Elijah's mantel, after the older prophet was suddenly taken into Heaven. When the timing is right, God will set up situations that cause us to step into our established call. And when He's ready to change things, there is not a man alive or any devil in Hell who can stop what God has said He will do.

UNDERSTANDING THE NEED TO STIR UP THE GIFTS

In the Scriptures, we're encouraged to stir up the gifts God has given to us, for many times they lie dormant. Peter wrote to the early Church:

Give diligence to make your calling and election sure.

2 Peter 1:10

> **Using our God-given gifts is releasing the anointing that is within us!**

Our skills are normally tied in with our gifts, and each skill God has given us should be developed with excellence. There are seasons in which one or more gifts seem to come more to the forefront than others. At times, this changes, as new gifts are developed.

Certain leaders seem to bring out, or help to develop, different gifts in us. Thank God for such people.

When God directs, we must never be afraid to use our gifts. The use of these gifts should make an impact on the Kingdom—in the marketplace, the church, or anywhere God has placed us. We must walk without fear of man in the power and authority of what God has said, and we must always operate with love. Using our God-given gifts is releasing the anointing that is within us.

UNDERSTANDING BEING DIFFERENT

God is into doing new things and doing them in new and different ways. It's easy for someone to question what others are doing when they've not seen it done in that way before, but we must not limit God.

Many times God uses what is familiar and, therefore, easily overlooked. For instance, He asked Moses what was in his hand. It was his old faithful staff. For Moses, that humble rod, so familiar to him, became, as we have noted, *"the rod of God"* (Exodus 4:20) because it was used to work miracles.

Elisha carried a mantle that represented the power of God. It was passed down to him from Elijah.

David was given armor to wear when he volunteered to fight the giant, but he gave it back. It didn't fit him, and he wasn't familiar with it. Instead, he used his already-proven skill with his trusted sling shot to win against the giant. This simple act brought about a new season in his life.

God handles the call differently with each person, according to the abilities He has given each one, and the situations into which He has placed each of us. Trust Him.

UNDERSTANDING DISTRACTIONS

In order to fulfill the call of God, we must not lose sight of the vision. Many, if not most, other people will not be able to see or understand what God has said to you. Even

Christians and close loved ones will unintentionally bring trials upon you by not understanding your call. You will be faced with spiritual warfare, with its power struggles and attempt at control over you, because the enemy of your soul always tries to interfere with God's plan.

Some of our most difficult tests can come through our own failures. The adversary will never roll out a red carpet to welcome God's plan. Instead, he sends people and things to distract us and keep us from focusing on our goal. When we somehow fail God, it always brings discouragement, and this can cause us to keep looking back rather than forward.

When we remain faithful during such struggles, there is a depth of wisdom that becomes ours through the process. Restless waiting and seemingly shattered hopes and dreams can actually cause us to connect more closely with the heart of God. All attempt to turn us aside can actually bring us back to the altar to seek God's presence and direction. Therefore, when we're obedient, God's plan always wins out.

UNDERSTANDING HURTS

Whether you're a leader, or just a servant, the altar is the place to lay down all hurts and to allow God's healing to flow to you. Unresolved hurts bring bitterness and resentment and can cause you to lose sight of the call.

There will be many trips to the altar before your call is established. And, once the call *is* established, the altar cannot be bypassed. The heart must remain faithful and pure, and it is at the altar of God that we receive His touch.

UNDERSTANDING DISCOURAGEMENT

All of us become restless when there are many obstacles to our success in ministry, and it seems to take far too long for that success to come. If our trust in God wavers when things look impossible, discouragement can set in. When that happens, we may begin to question our call and wonder if we really heard from God in the first place. Sadly, some actually fall away from God when their established call does not happen as soon as they expect it should.

We have a responsibility to follow God's leading, but it's not up to us to make the call happen. We must continually seek Him and believe that He will do what He has said He will do. And, in humility, we must die to self and allow Him to change us so that we are more pliable in His hands, able to become exactly what He wants.

You may have to do what David did. When there was no one to encourage him, he encouraged himself. [1] Trusting God for encouragement, he drew from what he had within his own spirit.

UNDERSTANDING BEING WILLING TO LET GO

Abraham waited for years for the promise of a child. Then, after that miracle finally happened and Isaac was born, God tested Abraham in the most severe way. If God required it, Abraham had to be willing to give Him what was most important to him, and what was most important to him was his son.

Amazingly, Abraham was ready to sacrifice that miracle child on the altar. But then God stopped him and showed him a ram caught in the bushes. [2] It was the perfect substitute. In this way, Abraham passed the test. He was willing to give God everything, so he got back his son, and he knew he could count on God's blessing and favor.

Understanding the Never-Ending Nature of Your Call

Seasons change, but the call never ends. Things may look different, as God uses you in different ways in different seasons of your life. But the purposes of God in your life will continue until you have taken your last breath in this world and have passed on to your eternal reward. What will be said of you then? The psalmist David declared:

> *The righteous will flourish like a palm tree.*
> *They will still bear fruit in old age,*
> *they will stay fresh and green.*
>
> Psalm 92:12 and 14, NIV

Let these words be your testimony today.

SAY YES TO GOD

Say *yes* to God. The most miserable person in the world is the one who is running from God and from His calling. Why should He have to raise up someone else? He has you. His Holy Spirit can teach you all that you need to know to be successful, as you faithfully follow His leading.

You are called to be a mighty man or woman of God, and that call is not limited to performing some role within the Church. Your gifts and skills are to be used in the world at large, as well as in the Church, so that God's full plan can be fulfilled in your life. From this day forward, expect signs and wonders to follow you. Become a history maker, and impact your world for Christ.

CHAPTER 11

WHY I WROTE THIS BOOK

And we know that all things work together for good to them that love God, to them who are the called according to his purpose. Romans 8:28

Some may wonder why I wrote this book or with what authority I speak on this subject. After all, my primary work at this writing is still in the secular world, or as I like to call it, the marketplace. I am giving more and more time to ministry, but I still have not achieved the level of ministry I've always envisioned.

But that is precisely the point of the book. We each have a special call, and reaching the fulfillment of that call takes time and requires a growing and learning process. My process may be different from yours, but each of us is working toward an ultimate destiny in God. My journey in life has taken me places I didn't anticipate going, but each step brings me closer to my final destination.

THE GODLY INFLUENCE OF MY PARENTS

> *That original calling is just as real today as it was way back then!*

My parents lived a wonderful Christian life before me and taught me how to pray, and yet they could not cause me to walk in my calling or even give me that calling. When I was ten, a missionary came to our church, and what he had to say so stirred my heart that I suddenly knew I was called.

My calling, first of all, was to win souls (a call that every Christian has), but I was also called to go into the world at a very different level, taking the message of the Gospel to those who needed it most. The Lord also put it into my heart at that early age that I would lay hands on the sick and see them recover.

As I look back on it now, it's amazing to think of just how many things the Lord put into the heart of a ten-year-old girl.

That call never left me. It's just as real today as it was way back then.

WHY I WROTE THIS BOOK

LEVELS OF TRAINING

As I was growing up, I did different things in the church. For instance, at one point, I was a youth leader, and at another time, I was in children's ministry. I sensed that each thing I was doing was just another step in preparing me for my ultimate destiny.

When it came time to go to college, I chose Southwestern Assemblies of God College in Waxahachie, Texas. I wanted to get a missions degree. Some way and somehow, I intended to become part of missionary work that would change the world for Christ. This, I knew, was my destiny.

MY COLLEGE YEARS

During my college years, I had many opportunities to learn and also to put into practice what I was learning. Again, I sensed that I was taking steps toward my ultimate ministry.

After I had finished four years of college training, I (along with others of my class) still needed one more class to complete my requirements, but the college was not offering that semester a class that would meet my need. I prayed about this. My prayer was answered when a notice was posted for a new class on the healing ministry. Somehow I sensed that this class had been set up just for me and that I should take it. After that original call I had received at the age of ten (letting me know that I would lay hands on the sick and see them recover), I had received visions confirming this ministry. Now I had a chance to learn more about it.

I wasn't disappointed. It was a wonderful class, one that stirred my soul more than anything else I had studied in those years. At the end of the semester, I wrote a term paper on the healing ministry, and my studies in preparation for that term paper only added to the gift being stirred up within me. God was getting me ready for something great.

MARRIAGE AND CHILDREN

I had worked hard and received a BS degree in missions, but now what? For the moment, some personal issues had complicated my life.

I met Albert Cummings in Bible college, and we were married between my sophomore and junior years. By the time I took that wonderful class on healing, I was already expecting our first child. Two months after I graduated, I gave birth to Michael.

That, of course, changed everything. Instead of reaching the world for Christ, I suddenly found myself changing diapers and nursing a baby. As any mother knows, taking care of small children is a full-time job, and with my new responsibilities as wife and mother, everything else had to be put on hold.

GETTING INTO MEANINGFUL MINISTRY

Upon graduation, Albert felt he had to take a job to support our growing family, and it was a year before we got into any kind of meaningful ministry. This was as relief house parents at Hillcrest Children's Home in Hot Springs, Arkansas. We were there for about a year.

We then moved on to another children's home, this one in South Texas, and we stayed there for the next ten years. About two years into our stay, our daughter Angela was born. My world was becoming ever more complicated.

At various times, I pondered this dilemma. Would I ever be able to fulfill what was in my heart? As I look back on it now, I realize that all of this was part of the training. At the time, however, this was far from obvious. Everything seemed more like some major detour.

Working in the children's homes was rewarding in its own way, for we were able to love and to sow God's Word into the children under our care. There were also other ministry opportunities. Albert was actively engaged in prison ministry there in South Texas, and we helped pioneer a church and served as its associate pastors for a time. But South Texas was not the mission field I'd had in mind.

For the most part, I had to resign myself to "home missions." My husband and growing children and our extended family all needed me, so I rarely ventured far from home. Would my vision ever come to pass?

OUR MOVE TO LOUISIANA

After eleven years of mothering a house full of children, I was tired. More importantly, I had a yearning to have us all together as a family, just the four of us. Michael was already in junior high, and I was afraid that he would never know what real family life was like. I had been sensing for some months that a new season for us was coming. Albert, too, became a little restless, wishing that we could somehow move closer to his parents, who lived in Shreveport, Louisiana. These elements all lined up to cause us to decide to move to Shreveport and see what God had for us there.

We rented an apartment in Shreveport, and I noticed Michael walking around and around in the room we had designated as his. Would he be the only person sleeping in that room? he asked. When I assured him that the room was his alone, he got very excited. Later, when I tried to store some boxes on the top shelf of his closet, he protested. That was his room, and he only wanted *his* "stuff" in there. I had to laugh. Until then, he had shared everything—not only his room, but also his parents. Now, for the first time, he had a room of his own and his own private parents.

We found a good church in Shreveport and became actively involved in it, but then we both had to find secular jobs. A growing family required more income.

Where Did I Want to Go?

After a few years of secular work, my heart was hungry for more. The job I had was a good one, but now I resigned and went to work in the church office as the pastor's secretary and church bookkeeper (I called myself the Minister of Books). I desperately wanted to be closer to ministry.

I stayed in that position for four years, and I enjoyed serving the pastor, but I wasn't satisfied. Would I ever find the place of ministry my heart so longed for?

As I look back on it now, the secretarial and bookkeeping work at the church, although it seemed to be far from my calling, was just another step up the ladder. With every step, I was learning more about the church and its ministry, and every part of my experience seemed to be part of the driving force to get me where I wanted to go.

At times, that seemed to be my biggest problem. I wasn't sure exactly where I wanted to go. I just knew that I had a call on my life, but where it would take me I wasn't exactly sure. It seemed that it would require a great miracle to ever get me there. What I didn't realize at the time was that each step was taking me higher. It was all part of the process.

What I didn't realize at the time was that each step was taking me higher!

In the years to come, I was involved in many girl's clubs and in many women's ministries activities, and anytime I had the opportunity to attend a prayer conference or other special event, I went. Still, nothing earth-shaking seemed to happen in our lives.

A MANAGEMENT POSITION

I applied for and was accepted for a management position. I was given high expectations, but then there was very little training or guidance to go with it. The job was demanding and fast paced, and it seemed to me that I was living a nightmare for the next year.

During that time, I prayed desperately for the Lord to put me into full-time ministry. I wanted to get out of the world, so to speak, and get on with His plan for my life. I later repented of that prayer. God had me where I was so that I could do something for Him, and each job became an opportunity for ministry.

After a year on that job, I began to find my place, and I stayed for the next seven years and did well. The job gave me a lot of good experience and prepared me for eventually running a company. But my soul continually cried out for more.

THE SPIRITUAL BREAKTHROUGH

By the 1990s I had become so restless and discouraged that all hope seemed to drain from me. The years were passing me by. What would become of all the dreams I had in my heart? It began to look to me like they would never come to pass.

It was at this very low point in my life that the breakthrough came. Revival suddenly came to the church we were attending, and I was determined to get my share of blessings. I just couldn't get enough. I was there for every service and every prayer meeting. This time, though, it was different. Instead of trying to do more religious acts, I became obsessed with knowing and experiencing the presence of the Lord.

I'd had my religious list, and I knew who was right and who was wrong, but now those thoughts had to be discarded. In the process, I experienced an amazing amount of inner healing, and the presence of the Lord became, for me, a place of total rest. Instead of struggling to find my place in the Church, I just needed to bask in God's presence and experience Him. He would do the rest.

STRUGGLING CEASED

At first I didn't realize exactly what was happening to me, but as I rested in God, I began to receive new revelation, new spiritual insight, and new direction. Through the years, I had struggled in prayer to understand certain things and could not. Now, by just basking in the presence of the Lord, understanding of them came to me—so easily.

One of the things I had struggled with for so long was to understand exactly what the Lord was saying to me. Now, that understanding came easily. I knew. This changed everything. My spirit became calm and quiet before the Lord, as a whole new confidence overtook me.

THE RESTLESSNESS OF THE CALL

Suddenly I knew that God's will had been in action all along. He *would* do all that He said He would do. I just needed to recognize the process and be faithful to Him through it all. This was a dramatic change for me. Now, instead of seeking ministry, I sought God, and He began to open new doors of ministry for me.

> *I just needed to recognize the process and be faithful to Him through it all!*

MINISTRY WAS DIFFERENT

I had always enjoyed any type of ministry for the Lord, but now when doors of opportunity opened to me, it was different. For one thing, there was a whole new level of anointing upon my life. I hadn't necessarily turned up the volume on my voice, but when I spoke, there was an unmistakable authority associated with it. More importantly, people listened to what I had to say, sensing that it came from God. He was doing the work.

I WAS STILL FAR FROM PERFECT

This is not to say that I was somehow perfect. I was far from it. At times, I would feel like such a failure that I would run to the altar and cry out to God. There always seemed to be something that was attempting to push me back, just when things were looking up.

184

Later, I came to realize that sometimes what I thought of as being pushed back was nothing more than a timing issue. The Lord was protecting me from trying to cause something to happen in my own strength, which could have been disastrous.

LETTING GO OF CERTAIN RELATIONSHIPS

As I spent more time in God's presence, I became aware of the fact that I had to let go of certain relationships. Certain friends did not necessarily pull me down, but they did keep me from moving forward. I needed people strategically placed in my life, people from whom I could draw supernatural strength.

Everything about my life was changing. My whole thinking process was now different.

MY PRAYER LIFE CHANGED AND THE SCRIPTURES CAME ALIVE

My prayer life was dramatically changed. Rather than telling God what I wanted, I now spent time getting to know His heart so that I could agree with His plans.

In the same way, suddenly the Scriptures came alive for me. I had been a teacher in the church all those years, but now the Scriptures had new meaning for me, and my teaching changed, taking on new life and becoming more effective.

MY MISSION TRIPS

To this point, I've been on a dozen missions trips—ten of them to Mexico, one to Honduras, and one to Romania.

I got connected with a group that was taking teams

into Mexico. These teams were made up of members from several states and churches. The principle mission of the teams was to do church building construction, but while the others built during the day, I was able to work with women and children and to do street ministry. Then, at night, we all joined in evangelistic crusades in the surrounding areas. I had the opportunity to speak for some of the crusade services, and I always prayed with the people who came around the altars.

The trip to Honduras was with the Louisiana District Women's Ministries. The mission was to set up medical clinics, but again, we did children's crusades during the day and held special services at night.

Later, I went with this same group into Romania, and that trip was one of the highlights of my life. We held ladies' conferences in three different Romanian cities and did other special services, and I was privileged to be one of the teachers for the conferences. My favorite point of every service was the altar call, when I could see needy people saved and healed.

These experiences changed me and created within me an even greater desire to share with others all that is in my heart. My heart has always been for missions, and I plan to continue these endeavors around the world.

My Writing

When I was about twelve, someone gave me a diary for a gift. I thought it was the neatest thing, and I began to write in it on a regular basis.

My diary entries were usually short and to the point,

and unlike other girls, I never wrote about boys or gossip. Instead, I always wrote about what the Lord had been doing for me. This caused me to focus more on what He was doing so that I could write it down correctly.

I did this off and on through junior and senior high school. Then, when I went to college, I began writing short letters to my parents. They enjoyed them a lot, and once, when I went home for vacation, I found one of the letters posted on a bulletin board. They all thought it was rather funny because it was only two lines long. I had just been writing to say hi to them.

From time to time, I would write poems or short articles. Later, I began to write what I called *Bits of My Life*. These were personal accounts of things I felt were significant and showed how God had been proving Himself to me over the years.

At times, I was encouraged to send some of my stories to Christian magazines. A healing testimony that I submitted was published in the *Pentecostal Evangel*, and because of that, I was contacted, and it was later published in the book, *Acts Today: Signs & Wonders of the Holy Spirit* [Harris, Ralph W., (1995: Springfield, Missouri, Gospel Publishing House)]. At times, I seemed to be writing because I had so much to say and I felt that no one was listening.

Then, in the 1990s, when that revival broke out in our church, I felt that I had to keep a Revival Journal so that I would never forget what God had done and how He had changed me. Whenever I have looked back at the entries in that journal, it has given me renewed faith, and I cannot help but weep as I relive each account.

Since then, I have filled files with sermons, teachings, and articles that I have long known in my spirit would someday fill the pages of Christian books. To actually write a book, however, proved to be a lot more work than jotting down some notes or writing a sermon. I had it in my heart to write books for years but couldn't seem to get started. The triggering event came when a pastor friend gave me a word from God and encouraged me to start. It released in me what was needed to begin this new season.

I now realize that writing has always been in my spirit and is a part of my calling. It's interesting to me to note that I have come from writing two-line letters to reaching into the depths of my spirit, knowing that the message that comes forth is yet another way to bring life to this dying world. Thank God for the privilege!

LIMITATIONS BASED ON GENDER

When my spiritual awakening came, and I began preaching and teaching in a new and powerful way (and, because of it, began to receive outside invitations to minister), I also began to resent the limitations placed on me by Christian society because I was a woman. God knew I was a woman when He called me. This fact didn't matter to Him, but it surely did seem to matter to a lot of otherwise good Christian people.

In the end, this just drove me further into the arms of the Lord. I knew that if He didn't open the doors and do the work, it would not be done. I could not push my way in. Only God could do it for me, and He has.

My Present Position in Business

While I was working in the church office, I came to know very well our minister of music. Her husband was the general manager of a local company in Shreveport, and I went to work for him as his office manager. That was the management position of which I wrote a little earlier. It was a very hard job, but we seemed to work well together.

Then, only a few months after he had hired me, he left to start his own company (He and his wife bought two Merry Maids franchises). During the coming years, he offered to hire me several times, but I wasn't interested. It was a family owned business, and I felt there would be few benefits to my joining it.

After eight years, when I felt that it was time for me to leave the company I was with, he contacted me again. I turned him down again, but then, several months later, I woke up one morning feeling like the Lord was telling me to go to work for him. I called him, and we reached an agreement. I would now be working in the office of Merry Maids of Shreveport/Bossier.

> *I knew that if He didn't open the doors and do the work, it would not be done!*

THE RESTLESSNESS OF THE CALL

To my amazement, after I had been there only three days in the Merry Maids' office, I was hit with the news that the owner and his family were moving out of state to take on another, completely different, job. They wanted me to manage their Merry Maids business like it was my own. I knew little about running a housecleaning company, but it looked like I was about to get a crash course.

I was to be the financial manager for the business. This included doing the bookkeeping, taking care of the accounts payable and payroll and making all other financial decisions. I was also to be in charge of advertising and marketing and hiring and firing. It would fall to me to make cleaning bids, to take care of public relations for the firm and to deal with whatever else might come up. I would be managing fifteen to twenty employees who cleaned some sixty houses each week. I had a lot to learn, and I had to learn it fast.

Since one of my many hats was to do cleaning bids, this required that I spend time in the customer's homes. I began to pray over people and their homes as the Lord put it in my heart, and He began to do wonderful things. Merry Maids of Shreveport/Bossier prospered.

This prosperity did not go unnoticed. The Housing Authority of the City of Shreveport contacted me, asking if I could begin teaching seminars around town about house cleaning. The seminars went well, and this led to me doing other things with the organization and to receiving special recognition from their state office.

Another group began to set up special classes for me to

teach, and I received an opportunity to speak for a local organization. I have also taken advantage of opportunities to teach for Junior Achievement in several of the public schools. After attending the Women's Business Council in our area (with the purpose of networking with other local business women), I was asked to be on their board and to serve as their program chair. I accepted, and this opportunity has caused me to interact with many business and community leaders in our area.

In the past year, I have been interviewed on a local community radio program several times about the company and about the Women's Business Council. Each open door seems to lead to another.

I recently told my staff that if we were in business only to clean houses, I couldn't stay with the company. Our office must be a place that radiates the presence of the Lord. We have a purpose and should make a deposit of God's glory everywhere we go so that we can have an eternal impact on our city and its citizens. Many people have been prayed for and encouraged through the staff of this company, and this will continue just as long as I'm there.

Because of all this, besides invitations to minister the Word of God, I also receive invitations to talk to church groups about ministering in the marketplace. Many of God's people want to bless those around them, and this teaches them how.

I'm not sure just what the next step will be, but I know that it will be a good one.

I have come to realize that it's not so much what we do that makes a difference in our world, but what we carry!

I have come to realize that it's not so much what we do that makes a difference in our world, but what we carry. The plan of God for our lives is in action—even if we fail to realize it. If we seek God and His will and are obedient and faithful, we can become a carrier of His presence. And that's what makes a difference in our world.

On a regular basis now I am able to minister to business people in the community. I'm sure that this would not have happened if I had only been working in the church or some full-time ministry. I knew very little about a marketplace ministry, but now I realize I have one.

RESTLESSNESS HAS LEFT ME

When spiritual renewal came to me, I began to realize that when the Lord was ready to do all the things He had placed within my heart, the anointing to do them would be there. For too long, I had tried to act out of a very low level of anointing, and it was a struggle to accomplish anything at all. Now

I knew that I had only to rest in Him, and He would do the work.

My hope was restored, and God brought to me a whole new level of courage. I was thinking in a whole new way. In the process, restlessness left me, and anytime it tried to return, I just ran back to God's presence to be reminded that He was in total control of my life. And it has worked. For the first time in many years, I am free from restlessness. In this peacefulness, there seems to be a higher level of trust. I know that God is in control, and I know that He will take me where He intends for me to go.

WHAT THE FUTURE HOLDS

As I look back now, I can clearly see the seasons of my life and the training ground each represents. This excites me because it makes me know that the future is glorious. I get excited with every new change that comes. Another season, another place in God, and it's all leading me to the establishment of my ultimate calling.

I am fully expecting God to fulfill the plan for my life, although I now realize that it will probably look far different than I ever imagined.

Why do I say that? Because nothing that has come to my life thus far has come as I expected it, and because I now know God better, I know that within a short span of time, He can (and does) turn everything around. Within a couple of years, I expect my life to be very different than it is today.

How About You?

How about you? Where are you in the seasons of life? What preparation ground does the Lord have you on? Please be assured that, wherever you happen to be in the journey of life, this present experience is just a stepping-stone to greatness, a milestone, if you will, on your journey to complete fulfillment. You, too, can overcome the restlessness of the call and remain faithful to God through the process of being anointed, appointed and prepared.

Even though I had a wonderful godly heritage, I've had to choose, along with my seven brothers and sisters, if I would continue in that tradition and leave behind my own legacy. Now I plan to pour into my grandchildren, Dylan, Dean, and Jacob, to encourage them to remain faithful to God while they're being prepared for their call.

As I close the message of this book, I wish for you the words of St. Paul's great benediction:

> *That the God of our Lord Jesus Christ, the Father of glory, may give unto you the spirit of wisdom and revelation in the knowledge of him: the eyes of your understanding being enlightened; that ye may know what is the hope of his calling, and what the riches of the glory of his inheritance in the saints, and what is the exceeding greatness of his power to us-ward who believe, according to the working of his mighty power.* Ephesians 1:17-19

Amen!

ENDNOTES

ENDNOTES FOR CHAPTER 1

1. Genesis 35:22
2. Genesis 49:28
3. Genesis 35:24
4. Genesis 32:24-28 and 35:15
5. Genesis 49:27
6. Judges 20-21
7. 1 Samuel 9:1
8. Genesis 33:18
9. 1 Samuel 8
10. Deuteronomy 17:14
11. 1 Samuel 9-11
12. 1 Samuel 9-11
13. 1 Samuel 15
14. 1 Samuel 14:47
15. 1 Samuel 14:52
16. 1 Samuel 10:8
17. 1 Samuel 11:15
18. 1 Samuel 15:35
19. 1 Samuel 16:2
20. 1 Samuel 16:13-14
21. 1 Samuel 16:14
22. 1 Samuel 17-31
23. 1 Samuel 18:8-9
24. 1 Samuel 28:7-9
25. 1 Samuel 31:1-6

ENDNOTES FOR CHAPTER 2

1. 1 Samuel 16:9-13
2. 1 Samuel 16:1-13
3. 1 Samuel 16-20
4. 1 Samuel 21-30
5. 1 Samuel 23:17
6. 1 Samuel 24:20 and 26:25
7. 1 Samuel 27
8. 1 Samuel 30:26-31
9. 1 Samuel 25:1
10. 1 Samuel 31:1-7
11. 2 Samuel 1-5
12. 2 Samuel 2
13. 2 Samuel 2-4
14. 2 Samuel 5:1-10
15. 2 Samuel 7:8
16. 1 Samuel 16:12-13
17. 1 Samuel 24:20
18. 1 Samuel 23:17
19. 2 Samuel 5:2
20. 1 Samuel 23:14, 2 Samuel 7:9, 8:6 and 14
21. 2 Samuel 5:10
22. 2 Samuel 11-12:25

ENDNOTES FOR CHAPTER 3

1. 2 Samuel 15:25
2. 2 Samuel 7:12-17

3. 2 Samuel 7:22

4. 1 Kings 3:3

5. Numbers 20:7-12

6. Numbers 20:6-11

ENDNOTES FOR CHAPTER 4

1. 1 Kings 19:4-21
2. 2 Kings 2:1-15
3. 2 Kings 6:12-17
4. 2 Kings 3:15
5. 2 Kings 8:11-12

ENDNOTES FOR CHAPTER 10

1. 1 Samuel 30:6
2. Genesis 22:9-13

ENDNOTES FOR CHAPTER 5

1. 2 Kings 4:8-37
2. 2 Kings 8:1-6
3. 2 Kings 5

ENDNOTES FOR CHAPTER 7

1. Genesis 12:1-8
2. Genesis 18:18
3. Genesis 12:10-17
4. Genesis 12:18-20
5. Genesis 13:3-4
6. Genesis 17:5-17
7. Genesis 20:1-2
8. Genesis 20:3-18
9. Genesis. 21:5
10. Isaiah 41:8

ENDNOTES FOR CHAPTER 9

1. 1 Samuel 16:14
2. Genesis 20:7-17
3. 2 Samuel 12:1-25
4. 2 Samuel 12:24 and 1 Kings 8:18-20

NOTES

NOTES

NOTES

MINISTRY PAGE

To contact the author for conferences, retreats, revivals, or other special services, use the following address:

Mary Cummings
SHEKINAH MINISTRIES
1144 Homewood Dr.
Shreveport, LA 71118
318-688-2289

www.ShekinahMinistries.net
Mary@ShekinahHouse.com